Angola's
last best chance
for Peace

An Insider's Account
of the Peace Process

Paul Hare

United States Institute of Peace Press
Washington, D.C.

The views expressed in this book are those of the author alone. They do not necessarily reflect views of the United States Institute of Peace.

United States Institute of Peace
1550 M Street NW
Washington, DC 20005

First published 1998

Printed in the United States of America

The paper used in this publication meets the minimum requirements of American National Standards for Information Sciences—Permanence of Paper for Printed Library Materials, ANSI Z39.48-1984.

Library of Congress Cataloging-in-Publication Data
Hare, Paul J. (Paul Julian), 1937–
    Angola's last best chance for peace : an insider's account of the peace process / Paul Hare.
      p. cm.
    Includes bibliographical references (p.) and index.
    ISBN 1-878379-80-1 (pbk.)
    1. Angola—History—Civil War, 1975- —Peace. 2. Hare, Paul J. (Paul Julian), 1937- . I. Title.
    DT1428.H37 1998
    967.304—dc21   98-29699
                                       CIP

Angola's Last Best Chance for Peace

To Alioune Blondin Beye
who worked tirelessly and courageously for
peace in Angola

Contents

Maps

Acknowledgments

Many people encouraged and assisted me in the writing of this volume on the Angolan peace process. I would like to thank particularly Chet Crocker, Jerry Bender, Mike Samuels, and Robert Cabelly for urging me to undertake this enterprise, even though the Angolan peace process was not completed and I continued to hold an official position with the American administration. Although being a player and writer at the same time might appear awkward at first blush, I actually found the two roles compatible.

I enjoyed enormously my year as a fellow at the United States Institute of Peace. I could not have asked for better support and cooperation from top to bottom. The congenial atmosphere was enhanced by the presence of so many stimulating colleagues in the Jennings Randolph Program for International Peace, who were always prepared to offer critical and constructive comments on what one was doing. Although many helped me in ways big and small, I especially want to thank Joe Klaits and John Crist in the Jennings Randolph program and Dan Snodderly, the Institute's director of publications, who constantly exhorted me to continue writing and not get bogged down in details. It was good advice for a novice writer. Subsequently, Nigel Quinney took over the task of putting the manuscript into final from. I have come to marvel at how skilled copyeditors actually are.

Most of all, I want to acknowledge the indispensable, constant support of my research assistant, Ursula Tafe. Quite frankly, this book would not have been produced without her. Ursula conducted extensive and well-organized research for this project and taught me in a thousand ways how to manage my computer, which was no mean feat. She also took a first cut at editing my drafts and offered critical comments on the product, which I almost always accepted. She did all of the work in drafting the maps, the chronology, and other sections of the book, as well as writing most of the first chapter. Beyond this, Ursula is an absolute delight to work with.

Finally, I want to express my gratitude to all of those with whom I have worked during the last five years to bring peace to Angola. They are too many to mention here, but they include representatives of the United Nations, Portugal, Russia, the Angolan government, and UNITA. They have been engaged in a noble task.

I accept full responsibility for the contents of this manuscript. In particular, I would like to emphasize that the views expressed here are my own and not those of the U.S. government.

Acronyms

ANC   African National Congress

FAA   Angolan National Army (Forças Armadas de Angola)

FALA   Armed Forces for the Liberation of Angola
             (Forças Armadas de Libertação de Angola)

FNLA   National Front for the Liberation of Angola
             (Frente Nacional de Libertação de Angola)

GURN   Government of Unity and National Reconciliation

MONUA   United Nations Observer Mission in Angola

MPLA   Popular Movement for the Liberation of Angola
             (Movimento Popular de Libertação de Angola)

SOFA   Status of Forces Agreement

SWAPO   South West Africa People's Organization

UNAVEM   United Nations Angola Verification Mission (I, II, and III)

UNITA   National Union for the Total Independence of Angola
             (União Nacional de Independência Total de Angola)

VORGAN   Voice of Resistance of the Black Cockerel
             (Jamba Voz da Resistencia do Galo)

Introduction

When the latest peace agreement to bring an end to the civil war in Angola was signed at Mulungushi Hall in Lusaka, Zambia, on November 20, 1994, the mood among the African dignitaries who had gathered to witness the ceremony was bittersweet. Though the president of Angola, José Eduardo Dos Santos, was present, Jonas Malheiro Savimbi, the controversial and charismatic leader of the major opposition party, UNITA (União Nacional de Independência Total de Angola), and the principal antagonist in the civil war that had engulfed Angola during the previous twenty years, was not. Instead, UNITA's secretary general, Eugenio Antonino Manuvakola, who had been the lead UNITA negotiator during the talks, took Savimbi's place at the signing table.

Savimbi did not come to Lusaka for one compelling reason. Following the initialing of the Lusaka Protocol (though not the formal signing) at the end of October 1994, the Angolan government had launched large-scale military operations that had captured several key provincial cities, including Huambo, the second largest city in Angola, situated in the heartland of UNITA-controlled territory. Huambo could be considered the "Jerusalem" of Angola because of its enormous political, strategic, and symbolic significance to both sides. In fact, during the colonial era, Huambo had been called Nova Lisboa, or "New Lisbon," and had at one point been intended to become the capital of a Portuguese empire stretching from the Atlantic to the Indian Oceans.

The government's military campaign was roundly condemned by the international community, which saw the action as a flagrant violation of the spirit if not the letter of the Lusaka accords. The American administration was incensed because it thought the Angolan government had made firm commitments not to engage in military operations against UNITA positions, especially after the peace agreement was effectively secured. Now it was doubtful whether UNITA, under such humiliating circumstances, would agree to sign the agreement after all. Although UNITA finally opted to sign, Savimbi chose not to give his personal seal of approval to an arrangement that appeared to be so shaky and that seemed to be stacked against him and his movement. He did not want to be seen signing a document of "surrender," even though if he had chosen to come to Lusaka, he would have received a hero's welcome by the assembled heads of state.

A deep pessimism, rooted in memories of the past, has always permeated prospects for achieving peace in Angola. The 1975 Alvor agreement, heralding an orderly transition to independence from Portuguese rule, rapidly collapsed under the weight of competing liberation movements and the intervention of outside powers. Much later, following the end of the Cold War, the loss of thousands of lives, and the destruction of much of the country's infrastructure, the Portuguese, assisted by the Americans and the Russians, midwifed the 1991 Bicesse agreement, which led to internationally supervised elections in September 1992. The ruling MPLA party (Movimento Popular de Libertação de Angola), led by Dos Santos, won the elections, but UNITA declared they were fraudulent, even though the UN special representative and virtually all but a handful of international observers asserted that the elections had been generally free and fair. The country soon returned to war.

In view of this history of failed agreements and virtually nonstop warfare, most observers thought it highly unlikely that the Lusaka negotiations would ever be successful. Once the protocol was signed, they questioned with some justification if it could ever be successfully implemented, especially in light of its rocky start following the government's military offensives. It is not difficult to be a cynic about Angola.

What lay ahead? Could Savimbi ever be trusted to give up the armed struggle since he had refused to do so after the September

1992 elections? Would UNITA stall for time during the implementation phase in order to rebuild its military organization? Was the international community prepared to put its full weight behind the peace process by authorizing the dispatch of a substantial number of "Blue Helmets" (UN peacekeeping troops), or would it take a wait-and-see approach? Could the hawks in the Angolan government be restrained? This last question had particular relevance since some of the government's generals believed they had had UNITA on the run during the offensive following the initialing of the Lusaka Protocol; they held that the army had been prevented from dealing a coup de grace only by its political superiors.

The distrust and historical animosities between the parties were simply too high, it was said, to permit any illusions that peace might finally come to the Angolan people. The dashed hopes of Bicesse cast a dark shadow everywhere.

Another frequently cited negative factor was that—unlike the case of Mozambique, for example—both sides in Angola had access to oil, diamonds, and weapons, and both had the ability to pursue war. Neither side was likely to win decisively if war were to resume. UNITA would be compelled to return to the bush, fight a guerrilla war, and hope the government in Luanda would eventually implode. The government, with its superior resources and manpower, could be expected to maintain control over the coastal regions and the provincial towns, but it would be hard pressed to crush UNITA or to keep the key lines of communication open within the country. While everyone could agree that renewed warfare would be ruinous for an already devastated country, the actors in the Angolan saga have not always followed rational (or Western) estimations of the "best" course to take. The parties tended to see the conflict as a zero-sum game and not, more broadly, as an outcome from which everyone could benefit.

The record of the negotiations in Lusaka also did not inspire great confidence. They had gone on virtually nonstop for more than twelve months, marked by stalling and bickering on both sides over issues big and small. Meanwhile, the Angolan government and UNITA had continued to acquire arms on a substantial scale and to engage in sporadic and sometimes intense fighting. The Lusaka talks seemed a sideshow, largely ignored or dismissed by the Angolans, the media, and the international community. The main drama was being conducted on the battlefields of Angola, where thousands of Angolans were dying of starvation or suffering from severe malnutrition. The United Nations estimated that a thousand Angolans were dying each day from war-related causes.[1] The situation would have been much worse if a mammoth international humanitarian assistance program had not delivered food, medicines, and other basic necessities throughout the country. And this grim picture only begins to reflect the reality of the situation.

Some observers have argued that the roots of conflict in Angola are essentially tribal, pitting the Ovimbundu ethnic group, from which UNITA draws its principal support, against the Kimbundu (as well as some whites and *mestiços*), who constitute the MPLA's power base. The now largely atrophied FNLA (Frente Nacional de Libertação de Angola) movement drew its strength primarily from the Bakongo people in the north. While tribalism plays a prominent role in Angolan politics, its significance can be unduly magnified, as a considerable amount of crisscrossing of tribal and racial boundaries occurs. Indeed, during the almost three decades of fighting, neither the MPLA nor UNITA ever really attempted to identify the "enemy" strictly along ethnic lines. Perhaps more important than tribal considerations is the geographic divide between the city and the countryside—that is, between the elites living in the cities and controlling the levers of power and wealth and the peasantry cultivating the land. In this sense, geographic, economic, tribal, and racial differences reinforce one another in creating a great divide in Angolan society. Savimbi calls his side of this divide *Angola profunda*.

Others blame the conflict on Angola's dismal colonial history and, later, the pernicious effects of the Cold War. From this perspective, Angola was a pawn in the hands of the superpowers, abetted by their proxies, the Cubans and South Africans. An ideological frame reinforced the internal divisions. On the one side, the MPLA, supported by the Soviets and by Cuban troops, espoused the principles of Marxism-Leninism; on the other, UNITA represented democracy and freedom, personified by Savimbi. In Africa, however, labels can deceive and mislead. To find a real African communist or Marxist-

Leninist has always been difficult. The same could also be said, until recently, about bona fide democrats. The asserted ideological differences separating the MPLA and UNITA have largely evaporated with the end of the Cold War as both parties, at least in principle, now embrace free markets and democratic institutions.

The prime motive behind the Angolan conflict has been the struggle for power and domination among, at the beginning, three—subsequently, two—liberation movements. The leaders did not trust one another and were unwilling to compromise. Agreements reached were quickly struck down. Indeed, early on, the liberation movements probably spent as much time fighting among themselves as against the Portuguese. Each movement had its foreign patrons, and this further froze their positions. Leading the weakest of the three movements at the time of independence, at least militarily, Savimbi actively sought compromise with Agostinho Neto (head of the MPLA) and Roberto Holden (head of the FNLA) during the negotiations with the Portuguese government that led to Angola's independence. But even Savimbi had to admit that he was not surprised by the collapse of the transitional coalition government, which had been agreed to prior to independence: "People tended to think that UNITA was naive to believe that elections would really be held. . . . It was not that. We knew that what was at stake was so big nobody was prepared to lose the battle."[2]

Yet after all is said about the cleavages in Angolan society, an Angolan identity and a sense of belonging to the Angolan nation do exist among its people, forged during the years of struggle against Portuguese rule. Ethnic, cultural, economic, racial, and geographic differences exist and are important, but they should not obscure the existence of this underlying, unifying thread, which can bind the Angolan nation into something better than it has experienced to date.[3]

PURPOSE

The purpose of this study is to examine the negotiations that ended with the signing of the Lusaka Protocol and the implementation of the peace agreement. The focus will be on identifying the key issues on the negotiating table, discussing how they were addressed, and describing how they were ultimately resolved. We will also explore the role of personalities in facilitating or impeding the peace process.

Breaking the cycle of violence and placing Angola on the path to peace required major external intervention. I will pay particular attention to the mediation mechanism, the UN secretary-general's special representative, and the "Troika"—Portugal, Russia, and the United States—that supported the UN-led effort. A central thesis is that while regional and other actors played a role in the peace process —sometimes positive, other times not—a single, strong mediator was the key to success.

Signing any peace agreement is only the first step; implementing the agreement can be more difficult. Fortunately, the Lusaka Protocol is a fairly detailed document and, therefore, less subject to ambiguity and differing interpretations by the parties. This has facilitated its implementation.

The nature of a peace operation, however, changes dramatically during the implementation phase. The number of people and resources required expands exponentially. Coping with a challenging environment requires true administrative expertise. Logistics often drives policy, rather than the reverse. Building a larger constituency committed to the peace process becomes critical. At the same time, the diplomatic and political skills so essential during the negotiating phase are still needed to guide the overall effort, provide an effective and authoritative interface with the key leaders, and resolve disputes and unforeseen questions and issues. In fact, the processes of negotiating and of implementing an agreement cannot be separated. They form a seamless whole.

The United Nations led the Lusaka peace process, whereas its involvement in the earlier Bicesse Accords was almost an afterthought. Once the Bosnian mission was turned over to NATO at the end of 1995, Angola hosted the largest UN peacekeeping operation in the world. Some have claimed that the Angolan mission is a "model" of how peacekeeping operations should be carried out. In view of the skepticism with which some people in the United States and elsewhere view UN peacekeeping missions, we will examine how effective the Angola mission was and what its relevance may be to other internal conflicts in Africa and elsewhere.

Finally, it should be noted that this study is written from an American perspective. I was appointed the U.S. special representative for the Angolan peace process in October 1993 and was involved in the negotiations in Lusaka and, subsequently from time to time, in Angola. Prior to this assignment, I was director of the Office of Southern African Affairs at the Department of State from 1979 to 1981, serving under the Carter and Reagan administrations. In 1985, I was appointed ambassador to Zambia, where I served for three years and came into contact with the leadership of the two principal liberation movements in the region—South Africa's African National Congress (ANC) and Namibia's South West Africa People's Organization (SWAPO). Although my direct contact with Angola was limited during this period, I observed the Angolan conflict from the sidelines.

This perspective may create a certain bias in the analysis of events and personalities presented in the following pages. But my objective is to describe how American influence and prestige can be employed effectively in a highly charged, multilateral context. The United States likes to regard itself as the "last remaining superpower," and for better or for worse, the rest of the world tends to see us in this light. This gives the United States certain advantages, which may or may not be exploited. I shall have more to say about the American role in the world in the last chapter.

ANGOLA AND ITS NEIGHBORS

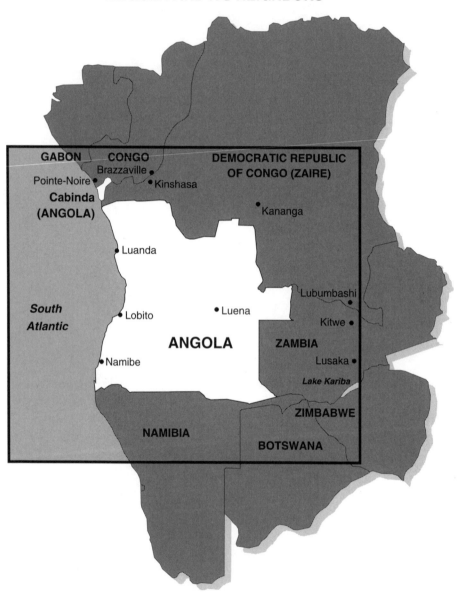

1

A Brief History

There is a story that Angolans tell: In the beginning when God created the world, he gave the best, most beautiful, and richest parts to Angola. And, according to the story, the rest of the world complained.

Angola is indeed blessed. From the central highlands or *planalto*, sitting four to six thousand feet above sea level, to the desert regions in the south and the long coastline abutting the Atlantic Ocean, Angola's varied landscape has a majestic, breathtaking beauty. The country is well endowed by nature. The land has good soil and river systems, making it potentially rich in agricultural production. It was once the third largest coffee producer in the world. Its oceans teem with sea life. Offshore, large oil reserves, created over the millennia from deposits coming down the rivers into the ocean, have been discovered and exploited. Oil production is increasing every year and will exceed one million barrels per day in the not too distant future. Within the land itself, some of the best diamonds in the world are found, as well as other natural resources, such as iron ore, marble, phosphates, and granite. Angola's people are hardworking. The land is underpopulated, with an estimated eleven to twelve million people in an area twice the size of Texas.

But the story of God's creation continues. According to the Angolans, God also placed a curse on Angola that its promise was to go unrealized. The root cause for this misfortune was attributed to the "bad" character God gave its people, who were figuratively scooped out of the bottom of the barrel and destined to misery and constant squabbling. Angolans tell this story with an ironic sense of humor.

THE COLONIAL LEGACY

In the sweep of history, Angola's tragedy began five hundred years ago, in 1483, when the Portuguese first established a presence on the Angolan littoral. The colonial period can best be characterized as one of exploitation of the land and its people, and the most destructive aspect of this exploitation was slavery. Of the ten million Africans sold into slavery, four million were taken through Angolan ports. When slavery was finally abolished in 1878, the exploitation continued through the system of contract labor. In fact, the entire economy was designed to enrich the imperial master, Portugal. The bulk of the population remained impoverished, uneducated, and powerless, ruled by a small elite of whites.

From time to time, the native Angolans rose up against their colonial masters. In 1902, the Ovimbundu tried to expel the Portuguese from their land in the *planalto,* but the Bailundo War, as this uprising was called, was suppressed by the colonialists' superior force of arms. The struggle for independence began in earnest in 1961. Although three liberation movements fought against the Portuguese, the real cause for the demise of the Portuguese empire was the April 1974 "Revolution of Carnations," carried out by disgruntled junior Portuguese military officers against the Caetano regime. Their first priority was to dismantle the empire, which by then was bleeding their homeland to death, because of the cost of maintaining the colonies by force and the resultant loss of life.

THE ALVOR ACCORDS—THE FIRST PEACE EFFORT

In January 1975, Portugal and the leaders of the three liberation movements—Agostinho Neto of the MPLA, Roberto Holden of the FNLA, and Jonas Savimbi of UNITA—signed the Alvor Accords, which provided a schedule and organization for Angola's peaceful transition to independence. But Portugal, too eager to get out of the colony, proved reluctant to become very involved in the decolonization process, and the agreement was never effectively implemented. The three liberation movements soon began to fight among themselves for control. Outside powers intruded and supported one side or the other, which further escalated the fighting and virtually ruled out the possibility of creating a compromise. The MPLA aligned itself with the Soviet Union and Cuba. The FNLA and UNITA looked principally to the Americans, Chinese, and South Africans. In the end, the MPLA triumphed over its two adversaries. On November 11, 1975, Neto proclaimed the independence of the People's Republic of Angola. Shorn of its U.S. support, the FNLA retreated into exile, while Savimbi regrouped his forces in the bush and eventually established UNITA's headquarters at the extreme southeast of Angola in a place called Jamba.

THE COLD WAR AND THE 1988 ACCORDS

Following its independence and throughout the 1980s, Angola became a pawn in the Cold War. The Soviet Union provided loans, military advisers, and weapons to support the MPLA government in Luanda. The Cubans sent troops numbering, at their height, fifty thousand. Although the passage of the Clark Amendment in 1976 prevented continued American military support to any Angolan group, including UNITA, South African forces crossed Angola's borders periodically to attack SWAPO bases in Angola—SWAPO guerrillas were fighting to liberate Namibia (South West Africa) from South African control. The South Africans also attacked Angolan targets in order to curb Soviet and Cuban influence in the region. If South Africa had not supported UNITA during this period, its chances for survival would have been slim.

While the war continued in Angola during the late 1970s and 1980s, the international community focused on Africa's last colonial legacy: Namibia. In 1976, the UN Contact Group—consisting of Canada, Great Britain, France, the United States, and West Germany—developed a plan that provided a framework for achieving Namibian independence, but South African objections kept it from being implemented right away.

When the Reagan administration came into office in 1981, the focus of American policy in southern Africa shifted. It now linked the Namibian independence plan to the withdrawal of Cuban troops from Angola. After the repeal of the Clark Amendment in 1985, the

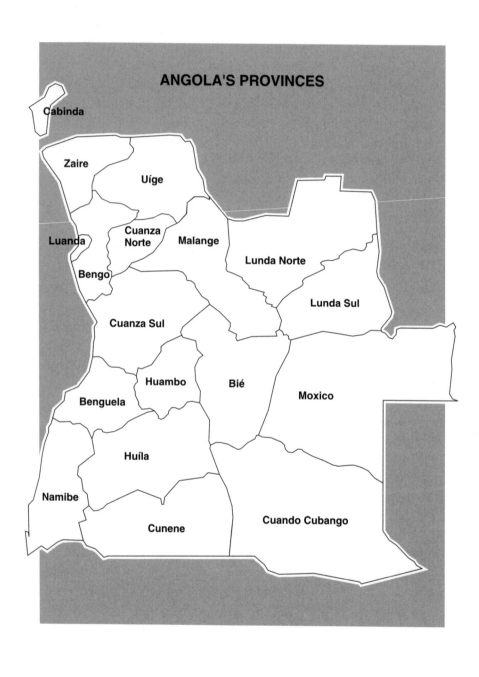

ANGOLA'S PROVINCES

Cabinda

Zaire

Uíge

Luanda

Cuanza Norte

Malange

Lunda Norte

Bengo

Lunda Sul

Cuanza Sul

Huambo

Bié

Moxico

Benguela

Huíla

Namibe

Cunene

Cuando Cubango

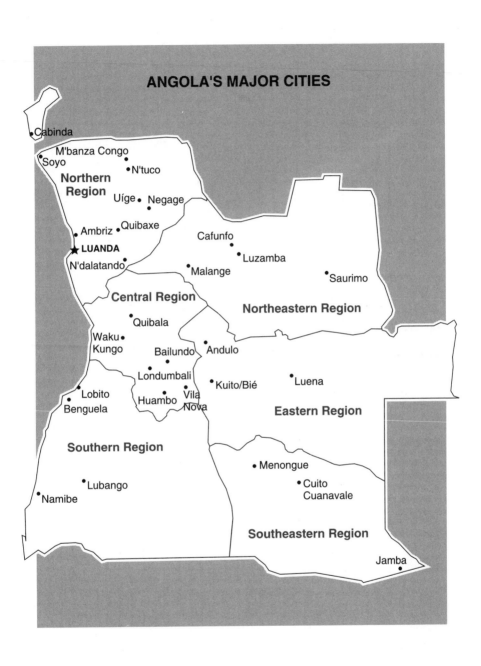

ANGOLA'S MAJOR CITIES

•Cabinda

M'banza Congo
•Soyo
•N'tuco

Northern Region

Uíge•   •Negage

Ambriz•   •Quibaxe

★ **LUANDA**
N'dalatando

Cafunfo
•Luzamba
•Malange
•Saurimo

Central Region

Northeastern Region

•Quibala

Waku•
Kungo   •Andulo
Bailundo

•Londumbali
•Kuito/Bié   •Luena

Lobito•   Vila
Benguela   Huambo• Nova

Eastern Region

Southern Region

•Menongue

•Lubango   •Cuito
Cuanavale

•Namibe

Southeastern Region

•Jamba

administration also resumed assistance to UNITA. Finally, after eight years of intensive diplomatic efforts and some bloody encounters on the battlefields of Angola, the 1988 Tripartite Accords were signed. The settlement provided for the withdrawal of South African troops to behind the Orange River as well as for Namibia's transition to independence. In conjunction, Angola, Cuba, and South Africa agreed to facilitate the withdrawal of South African and Cuban troops from Angola. On December 20, 1988, the Security Council established the United Nations Angola Verification Mission (UNAVEM I) to verify the withdrawal of Cuban forces.

While the 1988 accords succeeded in achieving Namibian independence and Cuban troop withdrawal, they did not end the Angolan civil war. A tentative step to resolve this festering conflict came in June 1989, when the president of Zaire, Mobutu Sese Soko, hosted a meeting of seventeen regional leaders. President José Eduardo Dos Santos, who had succeeded Agostinho Neto when Neto died in September 1978, and Jonas Savimbi attended. The talks led to the Gbadolite Accords, calling for a cease-fire between the MPLA and UNITA. But differing interpretations about what had been agreed to immediately arose, largely because Mobutu told the two parties conflicting stories about what had transpired. The accords were never implemented and soon forgotten.

THE BICESSE ACCORDS—THE SECOND PEACE EFFORT

Real progress in resolving the Angolan conflict came in 1990. At that time, Portugal, assisted by the United States and the Soviet Union, participated in a new round of talks with the MPLA and UNITA in Bicesse, Portugal. Motivating the negotiations were the simple but critical facts that neither side could foresee military victory and that their traditional patrons were now determined to push for a political settlement.

The negotiations were difficult but ultimately successful. On May 31, 1991, UNITA and the MPLA signed the Acordos de Paz para Angola, or the Bicesse Accords. A cease-fire took effect two weeks later. In addition to the cease-fire, the peace agreement called for the integration of the two armies into a single national army and the holding of internationally monitored elections between September and November 1992. The military forces were to be integrated before the elections. The accords also established what was known as the "triple-zero" clause, under which the United States, the Soviet Union, and Portugal agreed not to provide the combatants with lethal material and promised to encourage others to follow suit. At the request of the parties, the Security Council established UNAVEM II in May 1991 to support the process. Later, the UN mandate was expanded to include the observation of the elections.[1]

In September 1992, over 90 percent of the Angolan voters turned out to participate in their first democratic experience. When the final tally was announced, President Dos Santos had received 49.6 percent of the vote to Savimbi's 40.1 percent. In the National Assembly, the MPLA received 54 percent, while UNITA received 34 percent. Under the terms of the constitution, a second round of presidential voting was required since Dos Santos had not received an absolute majority. But this second round was never held. Although the United Nations certified that the elections had been "generally free and fair," thus giving an international seal of approval to the victory of the MPLA, UNITA declared that the election results were fraudulent. Soon thereafter, UNITA seized towns and municipalities around the country. Although UNITA gained the military advantage in the fighting that ensued, the government reacted by distributing thousands of arms to its supporters in urban areas. In Luanda, many hundreds of UNITA sympathizers, including some of its most prominent leaders, were killed in what came to be called the "October Massacre."

The United Nations and the three observer states tried to stop the fighting. At the end of November 1992, the United Nations held talks with representatives of the government and UNITA in Namibe, a southern coastal town. Good progress was reportedly made. But the mood of optimism was quickly shattered when UNITA violated the agreement and captured the important northern provincial capital of Uíge several days later. UNITA's leadership disingenuously claimed the attack was a "mistake," presumably the result of an over-zealous local commander and the lack of adequate communications with headquarters.

At the end of January 1993, a second effort was made to put the Bicesse peace process back on track under UN auspices in Addis Ababa, Ethiopia. While the initial discussions were inconclusive, the parties agreed to reconvene ten days later. But the UNITA team did not return to the negotiating table, citing problems with the security arrangements for their travel to Addis. In fact, their absence was due to a very different reason. A fierce battle had erupted in Huambo city, where the government was putting up a stiffer than expected resistance against a superior UNITA force. UNITA wanted to delay the talks until Huambo had been captured in order to give the party a stronger bargaining position in the negotiations. When Huambo finally fell on March 7 following a fifty-five-day siege, whatever promise the talks in Addis Ababa might have held to end the war had evaporated.

Despite these setbacks, the diplomatic effort continued. During April and May, then UN special representative Margaret Anstee conducted marathon negotiations lasting six weeks in Abidjan, Ivory Coast, which produced a draft document called the Protocol of Abidjan. Although the government delegation was prepared to initial the thirty-eight-point document, UNITA refused to accept a provision concerning the quartering of its troops. Its delegation maintained that any troop withdrawals from UNITA-held territories should be delayed until UN peacekeepers were deployed and could supervise the withdrawal process. UNITA also demanded that *both armies* be quartered, which meant that the two parties would be treated equally, as had been the case under the Bicesse Accords.

This position was a deal breaker. It was unacceptable to both the government and the mediators, and it did not conform with the various Security Council resolutions that had called for the withdrawal of UNITA forces from the areas occupied following the outcome of the September 1992 elections. An important issue of legitimacy was involved. Because the elections were accepted as "generally free and fair" by the international community, this meant that UNITA was in effect in a state of rebellion against the legal government of Angola.

With the collapse of the Abidjan talks, the prospects for resolving the Angolan conflict darkened. The civil war, which had raged largely unabated for twenty years, was responsible for untold suffering and misery. The statistics are staggering: 500,000 dead; 3.5 million men, women, and children who had fled their homes; a landscape littered with 10 million land mines.

Something had to be done to end this catastrophic human tragedy. In the next chapter, I will trace the steps that led to the third major effort to end the war in Angola.

2

Talks to
Begin Talks

I arrived at Lusaka airport on October 24, 1993, tired and suffering from a severe head cold after two consecutive nights in flight from Washington, D.C. Edmund DeJarnette, then chargé d'affaires and later our first ambassador to Angola, was waiting outside the terminal building. Several Zambian officials were also on hand, but they were behaving almost clandestinely for reasons that soon became apparent. As I was about to mark the box "official business" on the airport entry form, one of the Zambians told me in confidence and with knowing winks that I was supposed to state that the purpose of my visit was to go on a safari. The operation was codenamed "Zambezi Safari."

Just two weeks earlier, the assistant secretary of state for African affairs, George Moose, had asked if I would be willing to be the U.S. special representative for the Angolan peace process. He explained another effort was being made under the leadership of the United Nations to end the civil war in Angola. He did not know if the negotiations would succeed or could even be restarted, but he saw a flicker of hope, though he hastened to add that few others did. Moose indicated that the Clinton administration wanted to do whatever it could to support the negotiations that were being led by the UN secretary-general's special representative, Maître Alioune Blondin Beye. Congress also wanted something done. In an August 17 letter to President Clinton, Republicans and Democrats on the House International Affairs and Senate Foreign Relations Committees, and the chair of the Congressional Black Caucus, had urged the administration to appoint a high-level envoy, "with credibility on both sides," to the Angolan peace process.[1] The letter stated that the United States had important interests in Angola and the southern African region; these interests were being jeopardized by the war in Angola, and a strong American role was required to promote meaningful peace talks.

I accepted the assignment with some trepidation. I knew from my previous exposure to the southern African region that the roots of conflict in Angola ran deep and that many others more experienced than I had failed in their efforts to bring peace to this troubled country. But the lure of trying was tempting, even if the Reuters press clip describing my appointment was a bit daunting in view of the enormity of the challenge: "President Clinton named veteran diplomatic troubleshooter Paul Hare to aid UN efforts to arrange a political settlement in Angola and halt that country's bloody civil war."[2]

During the next few days, I was briefed at the State Department and the National Security Council and had meetings on the Hill. The most memorable encounter was with the chair of the House subcommittee on Africa, Harry Johnston. A representative from Florida, his candor and homespun humor were refreshing, if somewhat sobering. At the end of our conversation, he said, "Mr. Ambassador, I believe they have just given you a poisoned chalice!" In the weeks and months ahead, I often ruefully remembered Johnston's comment as we stumbled through the swamp of claims and counterclaims from the two Angolan antagonists. Following hurried briefings in Washington, I went to New York to meet with UN officials before traveling to Lusaka. Relations between the administration and UN Secretary-General Boutros Boutros-Ghali were badly frayed at that time over Somalia, Bosnia, and other hot spots. Angola had the potential to add fuel to the fire. There was concern that Maître Beye might wonder why the United States had suddenly decided to assign a special envoy to the talks. Would it be interpreted as a lack of confidence in him? Might he suspect that the Americans were planning to displace or circumvent the United Nations in the Angolan peace process? In view of the bad blood that existed between New York and Washington and the disdain with which the United Nations was viewed by many members of Congress, these concerns would be understandable. It had been agreed in Washington that my first priority was to establish a constructive relationship with Beye.

In New York I met with Jean Claude Aimé, an old friend and Boutros-Ghali's chief of staff, and asked if he would put in a good word on my behalf with Maître Beye. Aimé promised to assure Beye that the sole purpose of my mission was to support him to the maximum extent possible. This point was also made in the White House's announcement of my appointment. On the evening of my arrival in Lusaka, I met Maître Beye, who warmly welcomed me and the other members of the American team in his suite at the Intercontinental Hotel. Although Beye had only been involved in Angola for several months, he had an impressive understanding of the situation and was buoyed by an infectious enthusiasm about the challenge that lay ahead. After explaining what he hoped to accomplish during the preliminary meeting between representatives of the government and UNITA, Beye made it clear that in his view, the naming of a U.S. special envoy had been untimely, because it had led to undesirable publicity on the eve of this exploratory round of talks. He recalled that the two parties had talked constantly to the press, keeping nothing confidential, during the talks in Abidjan earlier in the year. He wanted to avoid a repetition of that scenario this time around. Hence the safari cover story. Beye also pointed out that the government did not want the prospect of renewed peace talks to affect adversely the morale of its armed forces, as had happened during the Bicesse period when its military machine had almost disintegrated. He thought the government might not send its delegation to Lusaka in view of the publicity surrounding my appointment. (The government team did arrive the following afternoon.)

In my somewhat rusty French, I told Beye that the United States did not want to complicate the negotiations. Our sole role, I emphasized, was to support him. Privately, I could understand why Beye may have been preoccupied by my appointment, but I also thought he was somewhat overstating the problems generated by the White House announcement. The effort to throw a safari umbrella over the Lusaka talks was bound to fail, since it was virtually impossible to keep out of the public view the procession of delegations that were descending on Lusaka's three main hotels. It might have been possible to maintain secrecy in New York or another large metropolitan area, but not in a relatively small African city. When I dropped by the Lusaka Golf Club to see some of my former Zambian golfing companions and told them with a straight face that I was in town to go on a safari, they burst out laughing. They knew only too well why I was there.

I was more concerned about how the Angolan government would perceive my role. It was quite possible that they might see me as a stalking-horse for UNITA in view of the historical links between the United States and the movement.

THE ROAD TO LUSAKA

The path leading to the Lusaka talks was marked by increasing violence within Angola and growing concern within the international community. Following the collapse of the Abidjan talks in May 1993, political pressure on UNITA had increased sharply. On June 1, 1993, the Security Council condemned UNITA for continuing the war, while it praised the willingness of the government to pursue a political settlement.[3] On July 8, the "Troika" (Portugal, Russia, and the United States) met in Moscow to assess the Angolan situation. In view of UNITA's military offensives, the Troika recognized that the government had a legitimate right to defend itself, which included acquiring arms. This declaration was important, since it effectively watered down the Troika's common commitment to the "triple-zero" clause, which had prohibited sending arms to either side. Although the Troika declaration did not specifically revoke the triple-zero clause and though it still stressed the need for restraint, it sent a strong signal of support to the government. The Troika also recommended that the Security Council consider imposing an arms embargo and restricting the overseas travel of UNITA personnel if UNITA's position did not change.

Faced with a steady deterioration on the ground, the Security Council on September 15 adopted Resolution 864, which stated that UNITA's military actions constituted a "threat to international peace and security."[4] Acting under Chapter VII of the Charter of the United

Nations, the council declared that an arms and petroleum embargo would be imposed against UNITA within ten days of the resolution's adoption unless the secretary-general indicated that an effective cease-fire had been established and agreement had been reached on implementing the Bicesse Accords and the Security Council resolutions. The resolution also stated that the council would impose additional trade and travel restrictions against UNITA on November 1 unless UNITA complied with the terms of the resolution. This was the first time that the Security Council had sanctioned a nongovernmental entity.

UNITA tried to avoid these sanctions. On September 12, UNITA's chief of staff, General Arlindo Chenda Pena "Ben Ben," declared a unilateral cease-fire effective September 20. According to General Ben Ben, UNITA took this decision in order to facilitate the delivery of humanitarian assistance and to begin negotiations.[5] UNITA's Political Commission issued a more comprehensive communiqué on October 6, following the imposition of the first arms and oil sanctions by the Security Council.[6] The seven-point communiqué reaffirmed the validity of the Bicesse Accords and reiterated UNITA's acceptance of the September 1992 elections, even though they were still considered fraudulent. The Political Commission also asked that UN observers verify its unilateral declaration of cease-fire. UNITA's communiqué and cease-fire declaration raised hopes that the peace talks could be restarted.

Why did UNITA decide to extend an olive branch to the government and the international community at this time? The imposition of sanctions and the prospect of more to come played a role, even though the arms and oil sanctions could not be effectively implemented. Without military force to back up the arms embargo, the two-way flow of diamonds and arms between UNITA-held territory and neighboring Zaire would be impossible to stop. Nevertheless, the sanctions did have political and psychological effects that extended beyond their practical application, for they increased UNITA's isolation on the international stage. If the second package of sanctions was adopted, the international travel restrictions that the sanctions included would be easier to monitor and enforce and would affect UNITA's ability to lobby and gather support from overseas.

The dynamics of the battlefield situation were probably more influential in determining UNITA's strategy (as well as the government's, for that matter). According to most estimates, UNITA controlled 70 percent of Angolan territory by September 1993. Its forces occupied important provincial cities, including Huambo and Uíge, as well as several strategic locations, such as the major airfield at Negage in the north and the diamond center of Cafunfo. They also had seized the oil town of Soyo. In the central highlands, UNITA had Kuito/Bié under siege.[7] Despite its battlefield successes, UNITA had created a long logistical tail, making it increasingly difficult to provide fuel and other critical items to its far-flung troops.

The government, meanwhile, had not been idle. It had purchased millions of dollars of arms and had hired mercenaries in an effort to redress the military imbalance. UNITA must have calculated that as the prize of Luanda itself remained beyond reach, the best course would be to consolidate its military position but at the same time repair its political image by engaging in peace talks. The announcement of a unilateral cease-fire was intended to freeze the battlefield situation, which still favored UNITA.

The government faced a different set of calculations. It needed time to rebuild its armed forces and to change the military balance; it did not want to be pushed precipitously into another round of negotiations. At the same time, the government was in a much stronger political position than UNITA. The United States had established diplomatic relations with Angola after the Abidjan talks had collapsed. The Security Council, as mentioned above, had commended the government's willingness to search for a political solution while it had placed sanctions on UNITA. Although these developments favored the government, they also made it difficult for Luanda to refuse to enter into new negotiations. On the eve of the Lusaka talks, President Clinton sent a letter to President Dos Santos that reflected the type of pressure being put on the Angolan government:

> While we share your hope that sanctions against UNITA can help bring it to the negotiating table, we were deeply disappointed that your government did not send representatives to the talks arranged in São Tomé by the United Nations Special Representative. I recognize that events over the past year have not encouraged the confidence

that is so important for the success of renewed talks with UNITA. However, I am convinced that it is only through direct substantive negotiations that remaining disagreements between your government and UNITA can be resolved.

I also recognize that current proposals for renewed discussions put forward by UNITA do not meet all the conditions set forth by the United Nations Security Council but I hope they can at least help the negotiations resume. I am pleased to learn that you have responded positively to the suggestion of the Secretary General's Special Representative to send representatives to Lusaka so that these proposals can be more fully discussed and clarified. Representatives of my Administration will be present to support fully the resumption of political talks in cooperation with the United Nations Special Representative.[8]

THE COMMENCEMENT OF EXPLORATORY TALKS

When the government delegation arrived in Lusaka in October 1993, they were wary and suspicious. The government's specific objectives were to obtain UNITA's unqualified acceptance of the September 1992 election results and its agreement to withdraw its troops to UN-monitored assembly areas, as had been demanded in Security Council Resolution 864. The head of the government team was the vice minister of foreign affairs, João Miranda, an experienced diplomat and excellent interlocutor. Miranda was not the government's usual negotiator, and this underlined the restricted mandate of his mission. In fact, the principal government negotiators were in Washington and New York during this exploratory round of talks in Lusaka. Other members of the delegation included General Helder Viera Dias "Kopelipa" and General Mario Placido Cirilo de Sa "Ita," national security adviser and chief of military intelligence, respectively. Both generals were influential and had the reputation of being hard-liners.

The UNITA delegation was led by Lukamba Paulo "Gato," who was in charge of UNITA's foreign affairs and was also considered to be a hard-liner. Two veteran UNITA negotiators, Jorge Alicerces Valentim and Eugenio Ngolo "Manuvakola," rounded out the team. All three were highly skilled debaters and adept at defending UNITA positions. Of the two key issues under discussion, Gato declared that

UNITA accepted the September 1992 election results "with reservations" that did not, however, invalidate the election outcome. He also stated that UNITA not only took "note" but "good note" of the Security Council resolutions, including the principle of UNITA troop withdrawal from areas it had occupied following the elections. Finally, the UNITA team insisted that the government should reciprocate UNITA's unilateral cease-fire so that the peace talks could be conducted in a peaceful environment.

The objective at Lusaka was to determine if there was sufficient basis to resume formal peace talks. After several meetings with the two sides, the mediation team realized that the discussions were treading water. Beye proposed a two-track approach to avoid being dragged further into what he described as an interminable "Ping-Pong" match between the two parties. UNITA would be asked to accept the principle of troop withdrawal to designated quartering areas, which had been the main stumbling block in Abidjan. The government would be asked to declare a cessation of offensive actions in order to comply with repeated calls by the Security Council to stop the fighting and establish a better atmosphere in which to conduct the negotiations.

When the parties met in plenary session, the UNITA delegation agreed to its part of the bargain and promised to put the commitment in writing to the UN secretary-general, which it did just prior to the November 1 Security Council deadline. Although neither DeJarnette nor I heard Miranda say that the government would declare a cessation of offensive operations, the Portuguese ambassador thought he had and he burst into applause. Maître Beye beamed. Formal peace talks, it was agreed, would begin in Lusaka on November 15.

MY PRELIMINARY ASSESSMENT

In my wrap-up cable on the Lusaka round of proximity talks, I provided the following assessment:

> I have been impressed by the dynamic, deliberative approach that Maître Beye, the Secretary General's Special Representative, has brought to the talks. He has been even-handed and vigorously enforced discipline on both sides. In the process, he has rankled feelings. One

member of the UNITA delegation said that he thought Beye's style undiplomatic, even brutal, a charge that I promptly rebutted. Beye has also been accessible and receptive to our suggestions, and has instilled a team spirit among the troika observers.

The gulf between the government and UNITA is huge substantively and psychologically. The government recalls UNITA's perfidy and armed rebellion following the September elections. UNITA underlines memories of the massacres in Luanda in late October last year. I have been particularly struck by the government's profound suspicions of UNITA intentions with regard to the peace process. They fear being outwitted in protracted negotiations and seeing the resurrection of UNITA's political image and military capabilities.

The two sides have starkly different interpretations of what is involved in negotiations. The government wants a pre-cooked deal, orchestrated by the United Nations and the international community, that would lead to a defanging of UNITA's military wing. UNITA wants an outcome that would give them political, security, and territorial space, a type of autonomy close to partition.

Despite these differences, the two sides have agreed to resume talks. They have done so because they realize that neither side can gain military victory over the other, though there are hawks in both camps who will argue otherwise. They are also forced by external factors. UNITA faces a resurgent government military capability (estimates of the extent vary widely among observers) and increasing political isolation. Some also believe UNITA is overextended and needs a respite from the war. The government feels trapped by the weight of the international community demanding a political solution to the conflict and the alleviation of the suffering of the Angolan people.

My cable offered some thoughts about the approach to follow:

The only viable negotiating track at this time is the effort led by the UN and Beye. We must repeat must give it our full support, bearing in mind that American backing gives Beye more weight and influence over the Angolan parties. This approach has certain implications. It may mean we will not always get our way on specific issues, though I doubt it will be a substantial problem. We shall also have to keep our rhetoric and public declarations at a lower decibel level than that to which we are normally accustomed.

We must make both sides realize that the international community expects, indeed demands, quick and measured progress in the negotiations. UNITA will be inclined to dawdle. The government will look to others to force UNITA to accept terms compatible with its interests.

It is imperative that the international community, and especially the United States, act with dispatch in the event an agreement is reached. This necessarily involves committing resources and money, bringing UNAVEM up to full strength immediately, and deploying soon thereafter a respectable peacekeeping force. Pre-planning and readiness will be critical in this regard. My initial estimate is that a peacekeeping force of 5,000 will be required.

Our levers over the parties will be strengthened if they are coordinated and orchestrated on a collective basis. With UNITA, it is the threat of more Security Council sanctions and increased political/psychological isolation. They still see the USG as the best guarantee of their security and human rights and would not want to see us disengage from the Angolan problem. With the government, influence can be best exerted by mobilizing diplomatic action from as many quarters as possible (and there are many). If the government balks at reasonable solutions, there is also the prospect of international disengagement.

This is my overview of the situation. Of course, the devil is in the details and the negotiating task is fraught with difficulties.

I concluded with the following thoughts about people:

I have an extremely strong team. Ambassador [Edmund] DeJarnette has been a bulwark of strength and wise counsel. Major [Richard] Fritz (Defense Attaché/Angola) and Dennis Hankins (Desk Officer for Angola) are outstanding.[9]

The exploratory round in Lusaka represented a diplomatic break-through, but the hard work remained ahead. The general principles to which the Angolan government and UNITA had agreed would now have to be translated into specific commitments and understandings. Each word would carry a certain meaning and implication to the two parties who had been engaged in one of the longest-running and most deadly civil wars on the African continent. There would be endless opportunities for hairsplitting squabbles that, though seemingly inconsequential, reflected the deeply rooted suspicion each side had for the other. While anticipating these difficulties, none of the mediators quite realized how difficult and protracted the negotiations would be.

3

Military and Police Talks

On November 15, 1993, Maître Alioune Blondin Beye presided over the opening plenary session of the Lusaka peace talks at Mulungushi Hall. Outfitted in a splendidly colored African robe, he was in a buoyant mood; now, after several months of intensive shuttle diplomacy, he would witness the fruits of his hard work. More than any other person, he had been responsible for getting the parties to this starting point.

Beye brought impressive credentials to the negotiating table. Having served as foreign minister of Mali for eight years, he was well versed in the intricacies of diplomatic forms and protocol, which may at times seem arcane but can be essential to the negotiating process. He was an accomplished jurist, which is why he was invariably addressed as "Maître Beye." Beyond its legal connotation in French, the phrase has another meaning—namely, "master," an implication that was not lost on the respective delegations or the observer teams. Beye also had "relentless intensity" and a strong positive attitude about what could be done, which some said bordered on being overly optimistic.[1]

An air of expectation filled the room. Beye and the other members of the UN team were sitting at the head table talking among themselves or busily shuffling papers. Behind them, the interpreters sat in their booths, presided over by their chief, Christian Pratt-Vincent, a Belgian of remarkable linguistic skills. The interpreters were the lifeblood of the negotiations since the participants spoke English,

French, and Portuguese but seldom all three languages. The three observer delegations were seated directly across from the UN table. Ambassador Yuri Kapralov headed the Russian delegation; Ambassador João Rocha-Paris of Portugal sat in the middle between the Americans (DeJarnette, Fritz, Hankins, and myself) and the Russians.

The UNITA delegation first entered the room, led by Antonio Sebastiao Dembo, UNITA's vice president. Dembo looked like a tough military officer. Prior to being appointed vice president, he had been in charge of UNITA's military forces in the north. Next came General Ben Ben, military chief of staff and Savimbi's nephew. Ben Ben turned thirty-eight while in Lusaka. Manuvakola, Valentim, and Gato had all returned as delegates, though their protocol rank had changed, apparently a frequent occurrence on the UNITA side. Other members were Isaias Samakuva, UNITA's representative in London; General Jacinto Ricardo Bandua; and Chipapa Kawendima, UNITA's representative in Zambia. A Portuguese lawyer, Antonio Augusto Oliveira, was also part of the UNITA delegation.

When Fernando Faustino Muteka, the head of the government team, arrived, he immediately strode across the room to greet his adversaries. The tension was broken. The other members of his team mingled with their UNITA counterparts, trading jokes and shouting out cries of recognition. The occasion seemed to be more of a reunion between long-lost brothers than the meeting of bitter enemies. It was surreal, as if the twenty years of bloody civil war during which countless lives had been lost had never occurred. Beye was delighted by the apparent warmth of the occasion. In his opening remarks, he referred to the Angolan "brothers" who had assembled in this room to bring peace to their homeland.

To an outsider, one superficial difference between the two delegations stood out. While the UNITA delegation was predominantly dark skinned, most of the government representatives were of lighter complexion, with the exception of Muteka and Miranda, the deputy foreign minister, who were Ovimbundu. Muteka was a former minister and provincial governor. His style was deliberate and calm, in contrast to that of his deputy, General Francisco Higino Lopes Carneiro, the mercurial spokesman for the team. Other members of the delegation were Miranda and Ita, who had participated in the

earlier exploratory round of talks in Lusaka; General Ciel da Con-
ceicaso Cristovao "Gato"; Ambrosio De Lemos Freire Dos Santos,
national director of the police; and Colonels Gilberto Da Piedade
Verissimo and Serafim Maria Do Prado. Lieutenant General Adolfo
Faulho Rasoilo was the delegation's lawyer.

MILITARY ISSUES

Following the adoption of the agenda listing the sequence in which
the outstanding issues would be tackled, the talks turned to the military questions. Major General Chris Garuba, the UN chief military
observer, chaired the discussions with the participation of the military attachés of the three observer countries. Major Fritz, who was
fluent in Portuguese and had extensive experience in Mozambique
and Angola, played a key role in facilitating the military talks.

The methodology of the negotiations was Aristotelian and often
difficult to follow. For each section or annex of the protocol, the parties would first agree on a set of "General Principles"; once that was
done, they would discuss the "Specific Principles" that flowed from
the general ones. The final stage was to work out the "Modalities"—
the most specific and at times difficult part of the process. This intri-
cate sequencing could, and often did, lead to convoluted and repeti-
tious statements and arguments involving subtle distinctions about
where various points should fit into the overall scheme. It also provided a field day for the lawyers, who generally seemed more interested in proving their legalistic mettle than in solving problems.
Drawing on his extensive legal background, Beye tore apart the
arguments raised by the lawyers, much to the delight and amuse-
ment of his observer colleagues. On the positive side, the parties
were required to provide their positions on each agenda item in
writing and in advance, thus highlighting where the differences lay
and suggesting how they might be bridged.

On the whole, the military discussions were straightforward, in
part because they were conducted by military men, who tended to be
more forthright and direct than their civilian counterparts. Dembo
and Ben Ben fit this mold. At one point during the talks, UNITA's
political representatives, Manuvakola and Valentim, intervened to

tell Beye and the observers that their military representatives (who were the heads of the delegation) had gone too far in agreeing with General Garuba on a certain point. Their intervention only served to slow down the talks.

In the military discussions, the first priority was to set down the rules for reestablishing the cease-fire following its breakdown after the September 1992 elections. It was agreed that during the first phase there would be a cessation of hostilities where they were occurring. Subsequently, as UN observer teams were deployed throughout the country, the cease-fire would be monitored and verified by the United Nations. The second phase involved the disengagement of government and UNITA forces where they were too close together and threatened to ignite hostilities. The objective was to move the forces some distance apart in order to avert a resumption of hostilities. The disengagement of forces was to be done in coordination with and under the supervision of the UN observers. These aspects of the military agreement did not pose major problems. The next phase proved more difficult.

THE QUARTERING AND DISARMING OF UNITA TROOPS

During the Bicesse period, the United Nations had sent military and police observers to monitor the agreement, but had not sent any armed peacekeeping units. Many observers of the Angolan conflict attributed the failure of Bicesse to a lack of resources and manpower.[2] This assertion had validity. In her account of her mission, Margaret Anstee had described her task as comparable to flying "a 747 with only enough fuel for a DC-3."[3] By the time of the talks in Lusaka, both sides recognized the need for a strong peacekeeping force to oversee the implementation of the Lusaka Protocol.

The primary mission of the peacekeeping force was to verify the withdrawal of UNITA forces to the areas where they were to be assembled and quartered and, at the same time, to monitor the pullback of government forces to barracks or defensive positions. This quid pro quo arrangement underpinned the entire withdrawal process. It was anticipated that the government pullback would ease UNITA fears that its forces would be attacked while they withdrew to the quartering areas. The two "Specific Principles" in the Lusaka Protocol describing this reciprocal arrangement stated:

> Withdrawal and quartering of all UNITA military forces (paragraph 8 of United Nations Security Council Resolution 864). UNITA shall provide the United Nations with updated, reliable and verifiable information concerning the composition of its forces, armament, equipment and their respective locations.
>
> The FAA [Forças Armadas de Angola] will disengage from forward positions under an arrangement that will allow verification and monitoring by the United Nations during the withdrawal and quartering of UNITA military forces.

The demilitarization of UNITA lay at the heart of the Lusaka Protocol, and just as had been the case in Abidjan, the talks nearly collapsed over this issue. Although the military representatives agreed on most points, they could not agree on the disarming of UNITA troops. The mediators (and the government) had taken the position that UNITA soldiers should turn in their arms when they entered the quartering areas. UNITA strongly opposed this proposition on the grounds that this would leave their troops vulnerable to government attack.

The mediators advanced several arguments in an effort to convince UNITA that the disarmament was a necessary step. First, under the terms of the agreement, the government's forces would be required to withdraw to defensive positions or barracks under UN supervision in order to separate the two forces and make attack less likely. Second, UN peacekeepers would be stationed at the quartering sites to provide protection and guarantee security to UNITA. If the government forces were to attack, they would have to advance through peacekeeping lines, which would have horrendous international consequences. Third, the United Nations would not deploy its troops around an armed camp and risk incidents, accidental or otherwise, that might occur. Beyond these stated reasons, the mediation team was not prepared to accept a repetition of the Bicesse experience when UNITA's military forces had retained their ability to fight. Nor did the mediators want to put the UN peacekeepers in potential hostage situations.

While these discussions were taking place, I saw General Dembo at a social gathering. He explained in his usual direct way why UNITA had difficulty accepting the disarming of its troops; he suggested that this point be put aside for the moment. Leaving the hard issues until the end of the process is a common negotiating technique. The "step-by-step" approach has characterized, for example, American diplomacy toward the Arab-Israeli conflict. The premise is that confidence between parties can be built up over time, thus making it easier to tackle the hard-core issues later, such as the status of Jerusalem. But I did not believe that this issue, because of its central importance to the peace agreement, could or should be deferred. If it was not resolved now, I did not see why it would be any easier to settle later. One could very easily slide into the familiar negotiating trap of wrapping up "90 percent or more" of the package but remaining stuck on one or two key points, as had happened during the marathon negotiations in Abidjan. I told Dembo that I did not see how we could defer addressing the disarmament question.

Later in the evening, I spoke to Valentim. Valentim could be loquacious, even strident—so much so that I had asked one of his colleagues if he could persuade Valentim to lower his voice during his frequent interventions at the negotiating table. Tongue in cheek, I explained that Valentim's discourses were hurting my eardrums! Valentim's counterpart and the spokesman for the government delegation, General Higino, also delighted in engaging in verbal duels with his adversaries. One simply learned to live with the windy outbursts of the two gentlemen, which were largely theatrical.

In private, Valentim, just like Higino, could be constructive and creative. He said that the real problem of disarming UNITA troops was psychological because it involved the sense of surrender and shame in giving up one's weapons. This was especially difficult for UNITA soldiers who had been fighting in the bush for years and knew no other way of life. He thought one way of resolving this dilemma would be for the UNITA soldiers to turn over their weapons to their commanding officers, who would then give the weapons to the UN peacekeepers. He thought this procedure would preserve dignity and honor. I told Valentim this was a good suggestion and did not see why it could not be incorporated into the protocol.

Beye shared the view that the disarming of UNITA's troops had to be definitively resolved, even if it led to an early demise of the talks.

The Portuguese and Russian ambassadors agreed. Faced with this unified position, UNITA relented and informed Beye and the observers that it was prepared to accept the disarming of UNITA soldiers at the quartering areas if it was done honorably. Valentim outlined his plan for the turnover of weapons, which was subsequently incorporated in the "Timetable of the Bilateral Cease-Fire Modalities":

> The operation to collect all lethal war matériel of UNITA's military forces will be conducted directly by the general staff and the command elements of these troops under United Nations verification, monitoring, and control.

This agreement represented the first major breakthrough in the Lusaka negotiations. During dinner with the government delegation that evening, I informed Muteka of UNITA's decision. He was surprised; he had never expected that UNITA would agree to disarm its troops.

The military talks concluded December 11 with the issue of the size of the revamped armed forces still unresolved. UNITA wanted to adhere to the Bicesse formula, which had limited the size of the armed forces to fifty thousand. Within this number, the army would comprise forty thousand men, and, based on the principle of parity contained in the Bicesse Accords, each side would contribute twenty thousand soldiers. Since UNITA did not have an air force or navy, its participation in these two branches would be marginal. Although the government claimed to accept the principles of the Bicesse Accords, it argued that the size of the military forces should be increased to 120,000 on the basis that Angola had long borders requiring a larger defense force. The government's real objective, however, was to exert greater control over UNITA by absorbing all of its forces into the army; this would, in effect, have made adherence to the parity principle impossible. Faced with this impasse, the two sides agreed that their military commanders would address this issue at a later date. Unlike the question of disarmament, the mediators believed this issue was not a "deal breaker."

The military talks had taken a little more than three weeks— longer than expected—but, as it turned out, they had moved at a hurricane pace compared to what was to come. Although Beye's hope of wrapping up the negotiations by the middle of December was rapidly fading, no one felt discouraged because the thorny question of UNITA demilitarization had been resolved, at least on paper.

THE KUITO/BIÉ INCIDENT

Just as the parties prepared to turn to the next agenda item, the talks went into a tailspin. UNITA announced that the government had attempted to assassinate Savimbi on December 11 during a bombing raid on the outskirts of Kuito/Bié, a key provincial town in the central highlands. General Dembo was incensed and declared emotionally, "The government has tried to kill my leader!" In view of the gravity of the charges, UNITA suspended its participation in the talks, though its delegation did not leave Lusaka. The government initially denied it had conducted a bombing raid, but this conflicted with eyewitness reports received from nongovernmental representatives in Kuito/Bié; eventually, the government asserted that the bombardments were in reaction to sightings of a UNITA military convoy moving toward Kuito/Bié.

Beye, Garuba, and the Troika ambassadors agreed that some action had to be taken in response to UNITA's allegation. A commission of inquiry, made up of the three observer military attachés and UNAVEM military officers, was sent to investigate on the spot. Several days later, they returned to Lusaka to report that there had been a bombing raid, but they had been unable to confirm the attempted assassination or even Savimbi's presence in the area. UNITA was mollified by the report, but more than a week had been lost in the talks.

The Kuito/Bié incident illustrated how the continued fighting in Angola could undermine the peace talks. Although the government had agreed during the exploratory round in Lusaka to stop offensive operations, it continued to conduct air strikes and carry out military operations. The mediation team condemned the air attacks, but its declarations had little effect. In tit-for-tat exchanges, the government claimed that UNITA was engaged in offensive operations, which was why it could not honor its commitment to cease hostilities.

Without a third-party presence, the charges and countercharges were impossible to sort out. The residual UNAVEM presence in

Angola was minimal, numbering only sixty-five to seventy military and police observers stationed in five relatively secure areas at some distance from the fighting. This severely restricted the United Nations' ability to monitor events. Over time, it became clear that the only way to stop the fighting would be to reach agreement on a global cease-fire monitored by a substantially augmented UN force. Rhetorical declarations calling for "maximum restraint" would not do the trick.

Although the government bore the main responsibility for the interruption of the talks in December, it is curious that the alleged assassination plot occurred just as the military talks had concluded. Had UNITA's leadership decided the talks should be slowed down and sought a convenient pretext for doing so? Given the state of art of the Angolan air force and the rainy weather conditions at that time of the year, the assassination accusation seemed a bit far-fetched.

POLICE ISSUES

The Bicesse Accords had not dealt with the police issue in any depth; now, in Lusaka, the negotiators recognized that this issue required more serious consideration. On the surface, it seemed relatively easy to deal with, but as the layers around it were peeled away, it became explosive and the negotiations grew protracted and often bitter.

Little was resolved on the police agenda before the talks recessed for the Christmas break. When the delegations returned at the beginning of January 1994, UNITA's delegation had changed. Generals Dembo and Ben Ben had remained behind in Angola. Manuvakola was now in charge, seconded by Valentim. The two explained that since the talks were now focused on political subjects, the generals were no longer needed. The mediators were not encouraged by this development, since Dembo and Ben Ben had been pragmatic in their approach, while Manuvakola and Valentim had a harder, more disputatious edge.

The most controversial item on the police agenda was the Rapid Intervention Police, often referred to disparagingly as the "ninjas." The Rapid Intervention Police, an elite force recruited from the military and trained and equipped by Spain, had been established by the government following the signing of the Bicesse Accords. The force was mobile and heavily armed.

UNITA maintained that the Rapid Intervention Police had been created illegally during the Bicesse period and now demanded its dissolution. Manuvakola and Valentim were vehement and emotional in denouncing the force, claiming that the "ninjas" had been primarily responsible for the massacre of UNITA sympathizers in Luanda and other cities following the September 1992 elections. The government insisted that it, like other governments, had a right to form antiriot police units, and vigorously defended the role of the Rapid Intervention Police. Muteka said, "UNITA had us by the throat and the only thing that saved us was the Rapid Intervention Police. They know it. That is why they are so angry." More than any other issue, the question of the Rapid Intervention Police rekindled bitter memories of the past.

The mediation team took the position that the Rapid Intervention Police had a legitimate role in preserving law and order but that its missions needed to be spelled out in the protocol so that they conformed to real police functions. Accordingly, the parties agreed that the Rapid Intervention Police would be confined to barracks under UN verification while UNITA withdrew its troops to the quartering areas. Also, the force's weapons would be adapted to specific police missions; for example, it would not have heavy weapons, such as tanks or armored personnel carriers. Finally, UNITA was told that the best way to create an impartial national police force would be to participate in the police structure at all levels, including in the Rapid Intervention Police.

This led to the second issue dominating the police agenda: the extent of UNITA's participation in the police. Like the merchants in a Middle Eastern bazaar, the parties started with their maximum positions. UNITA wanted to have 40 percent representation in the police force; the government offered 3,125 positions, or a little above 10 percent. Under the "General Principles," the two parties finally agreed that "a significant number of UNITA members shall be incorporated."

Bridging the numbers gap proved to be difficult. The mediators pressed the government to improve its initial offer and to increase the number of officer and sergeant positions. At the same time,

UNITA was urged to pare down its demands. After protracted discussions, the government finally agreed to increase its offer to 5,500 positions. The U.S. delegation said they had "squeezed the rock dry" in extracting this concession from the government. When UNITA countered with a final demand for 7,000 slots, Beye also insisted he could do no more and told UNITA he had given the government his word that he had come to their well for the last time. Through some clever statistical analysis, DeJarnette determined that the government could offer additional officer and sergeant positions within the 5,500 ceiling, which the government and then UNITA accepted. With this final compromise, the police chapter was closed on January 31.

EMERGING PATTERNS

The military and police negotiations had taken two and a half months, far longer than anticipated, and had made my bold affirmation that "Lusaka would not be another Abidjan" sound increasingly hollow. Although the mediation team constantly admonished the parties to make swifter progress, this pressure had little effect. Over time, Beye stopped issuing new calendars and deadlines because he realized how futile they had become.

UNITA was primarily responsible for the slow pace of the talks, though the government's insistence on its sovereign rights was exasperating and also caused delays. UNITA employed a variety of techniques to slow down the talks. Its delegation was almost always late for meetings (the government team was invariably on time). UNITA often pleaded that it needed more time to reflect on the complicated issues that were being discussed or that it had limited staff (unlike the government) to conduct the necessary study and research. Sometimes UNITA cited communications problems with its headquarters in Huambo to explain why it was unable to comply with yet another mediation deadline. As hours and days were lost, the patience of the mediators was sorely tried.

Why did UNITA delay the negotiations? In some instances, the excuses could be taken at face value. More practically, the technique was probably bound up in the time-honored tradition of trying to wear down the opposition and the mediators by stringing out the talks in order to extract additional concessions. If this was the intention, the tactic failed, since the government was prepared to play the same game. Some speculated that UNITA was not interested in an agreement but was simply stalling for time in order to better equip its forces, especially now that it controlled the rich diamond areas around Cafunfo. The most common speculation centered on the April elections in South Africa. According to this interpretation, UNITA wanted to see how the first multiracial elections in South Africa would turn out. If they led to the splintering of the state, as some predicted, this might open up new possibilities within the southern African region that UNITA could exploit to its advantage. UNITA denied this connection. In a speech on March 16, Savimbi said there was "no link whatever between the South African and Angolan problems."[4]

Given the paucity of intelligence about UNITA and the inaccessibility of Savimbi during this period, UNITA's motives were difficult to gauge. The only thing that was clear was that the negotiations were proceeding at a snail's pace and UNITA was the primary culprit. Despite this frustration, the mediators were encouraged that the military and police dossiers had been completed and initialed by the parties. The specific character of the agreements that had been reached reinforced the impression that the talks had a serious purpose and the parties were not engaged in an elaborate charade.

During the first two and a half months, a certain pattern had developed for the talks. The large room that had been used for the opening session was deserted, used only to ratify agreements already reached or to provide a haven of silence for a tired negotiator. Most of the talks were held in the smaller rooms of Mulungushi Hall where a more businesslike atmosphere prevailed. Although the two delegations would meet together at times, the mediation team would usually see them separately, which helped to reduce polemics. For more serious discussions, the mediators would meet with just the heads of each delegation at Mulungushi Hall or in one of the hotels. Beye and the observers employed every conceivable format during the negotiations, depending on their judgment of which approach would most usefully advance the process.

Beye was indisputably in command of the negotiations. Although the delegations might occasionally grumble about his strong-arm tactics and his inclination to impose discipline, they never got far in their complaints. The Troika observers stood solidly behind him. Despite occasional attempts by the parties to create splits within the mediation team, they did not succeed.

Beye was determined to preserve this unity among the Troika, which was not always an easy task. Even though he and the observers worked together on a daily, even hourly, basis to discuss strategy and tactics, differences emerged. The Russian position tended to be dogmatic and tilted sharply toward the government. In fact, though, with the end of the Cold War and demise of the Soviet Union, the Russians no longer had a major stake in Angola. Their main interest was to retrieve some portion of the billions of dollars of debt that Angola had piled up during the Cold War period.

The Portuguese ambassador, João Rocha-Paris, was an accomplished diplomat. Like DeJarnette, he spoke English, French, and Portuguese, which facilitated the dialogue considerably. Since Portugal was closely aligned with the Angolan government, Rocha-Paris had the difficult task of balancing Portugal's bilateral interests in Angola and the imperatives of the peace talks. If the two conflicted, he invariably gave the peace talks the higher priority. In the best sense of the word, Rocha-Paris was an "honest broker," who earned the respect, if not necessarily the approbation, of both sides. In the same March 16 speech already quoted, Savimbi declared that "the Portuguese Ambassador has shown extraordinarily good manners and the kind of understanding that is typical of a true Portuguese citizen who defends, in addition to the institutions he represents, the need for peace in Angola."[5] I could not agree more.

Because of their country's superpower status, the Americans carried a special weight within the Troika. Even though the traditional ties with UNITA had been severed for some time, the United States still had a certain degree of influence with that organization, at least to the extent that UNITA wanted to maintain its access to American officials. The Angolan government also wanted to develop stronger ties with the United States and maintained an active dialogue with the American delegation. Beye appreciated what the Americans could do and sought to use American influence in every possible way to advance the process. The relationship was close, productive, and professional.

Admittedly, the Troika was a creaky vessel and not an ideal mediation mechanism. Portugal and Russia were closely identified with the government in Luanda, and this tended to tarnish their image of being evenhanded. Despite these disadvantages, the Troika, which had been inherited from the Bicesse period, could not be jettisoned without revamping the entire approach to the negotiations. As long as Beye and Rocha-Paris provided an anchor of good judgment, the mechanism worked satisfactorily.

With the completion of the police dossier at the end of January, hope sprang up that the talks would move more quickly. With his usual infectious optimism, Beye thought the agreement could be concluded by March, based on the rational calculation that the bloody war in Angola had to be stopped and no major impediments stood in the way. The parties, however, had different priorities and timetables. So did their armies.

4

The Political Quid Pro Quo

The Lusaka Protocol involved a trade-off between two key issues. On the one hand, UNITA would disarm its military wing and become a legitimate political party. Its soldiers could either join the national army or the police or be reintegrated into civilian life. The UNITA generals would be incorporated into the military command structure, as they had fleetingly been during the Bicesse period. During this phase of the negotiations, UNITA was asked to make most but by no means all of the concessions. On the other hand, UNITA would be offered positions in the government at all levels—national, provincial, and local—and its deputies would return to the National Assembly so that the party could participate fully in the political life of the country and help to promote a spirit of national reconciliation. During this next phase of the negotiations, the government would be asked to offer political space to UNITA. The question was how much it would concede.

When the parties began their political discussions in Lusaka, a familiar pattern emerged. At the end of January 1994, the government captured Ambriz, an important town on the coast seventy miles north of Luanda. This military action was the harbinger of worse fighting to come. On February 5, Valentim issued a communiqué that strongly condemned the government for launching air and land attacks against UNITA positions in Kuito/Bié and the surrounding villages.[1] He laid the blame squarely on the shoulders of the chief of general staff, General João de Matos, who had made "warmongering" statements that the Lusaka negotiations were mere propaganda and that the Angolan people should prepare to live through trying times. On February 7, Huambo was bombed, halting the delivery of relief supplies. In retaliation, UNITA shelled Malange. The situation was getting hot. As usual, claims and counterclaims flew about who was responsible for the outbreak of hostilities. UNITA threatened to halt substantive negotiations if the government did not stop the fighting.

In response to the deteriorating situation, the White House issued a press statement on February 10 condemning the latest outbreak of violence and calling on the government and UNITA to "recommit to a total cease-fire."[2] Secretary of State Warren Christopher sent a letter to President Dos Santos on February 18, in which he said I had reported that the Angolan government "might pursue offensive military operations in tandem with the ongoing negotiations in Lusaka," which would undermine the "fragile framework for peace built by our joint efforts over the past four months."[3] The secretary hoped that I would soon be able to report that the peace talks had not been imperiled. Yet when I returned to Lusaka in the middle of February after a ten-day absence, I told Higino that the scheduled visit of the Agency for International Development team to assess how the peace process could be supported had to be postponed because of the government's aggressive posture. Never one to conceal his emotions, Higino replied that my comments made him "lose his appetite."

Whether these importunities had an effect is hard to tell. The talks did take a more serious turn, leading to an agreement on February 17 regarding the "General Principles" for national reconciliation. These principles were not in themselves particularly noteworthy. Most important was the provision granting amnesty for "illegal acts committed by anyone prior to the signing of the Lusaka Protocol, in the context of the current conflict." A leitmotif was the government's insistence that existing legislation be respected versus UNITA's desire to change the laws, especially with respect to decentralization or the devolution of power to local authorities. This led to awkward formulations such as "That, in accordance with Article 54 (d) and (e) and Article 89 (c) and (d) of the Constitutional Law of the Republic of Angola, the administration of the country [shall] be effectively decentralized and deconcentrated." During these discussions, we all became amateur experts on the Angolan constitution, though I believe only Maître Beye truly understood the principle of "deconcentration"! Only passing reference was made in the "General Principles" to the core issue: the extent of UNITA's participation in the government. One paragraph noted that UNITA would participate "adequately" at all levels of political, economic, and administrative activity, but that was all that was said on the matter.

The going got tougher when the delegations turned to the "Specific Principles." Although agreement was eventually reached on twelve of the eighteen specific principles, there was a stalemate on the other six, including most importantly the future status of the Voice of Resistance of the Black Cockerel (VORGAN), UNITA's shortwave radio station, and the return of the UNITA deputies to the National Assembly. The parties were working at cross-purposes. The government, hoping to gain maximum leverage, wanted to wrap up the remaining national reconciliation issues before addressing the question of UNITA's political participation. UNITA took the opposite view. DeJarnette and I became increasingly frustrated with the government's waiting game and told Muteka and Higino the time had come to start discussions of the positions that would be offered to UNITA. Beye had also concluded that the negotiations had come to a dead end and that this core issue on the political agenda needed to be addressed. João Rocha-Paris and Mikhail Botcharnikov, the Russian ambassador in Zambia, concurred.[4]

The government finally relented. On March 3, the question of UNITA's participation was put on the table. By this time, the mediators had decided that this issue should be discussed directly between the parties without anyone else in the room. The mediation team did not want to be caught once again in the crossfire of interminable haggling that had occurred when the status of the police had been discussed. More fundamentally, Beye and the observers thought it would be difficult for outsiders, such as themselves, to understand fully the intricacies and nuances of such politically sensitive issues. Yet it was also essential that the mediators know what had actually transpired in the discussions, since different accounts had circulated when this subject was discussed privately between the parties in Abidjan. The mediation team insisted this time that the leaders of the two delegations would give a joint report of what had been discussed and agreed.

The approach floundered almost immediately. The parties soon reported that they had failed to find common ground and asked the mediation team to intervene. The mediators had little choice but to become involved, though the prospect of bridging the gap looked bleak. UNITA had signaled much earlier that it wanted a power-sharing arrangement amounting virtually to an equal division of spoils among the ministries at the national level, including three important portfolios: defense or interior, finance or home affairs, and foreign affairs or information. The government had countered with three relatively unimportant ministries, five vice ministerial positions, and one provincial governor position, as well as a limited number of local positions.

MARCH 10 PROPOSALS

Making it clear that the government's initial offer was inadequate, Beye and the observers first conferred with that delegation about ways to improve its offer. Most of the discussion focused on what positions should be offered at the national level; much less attention was given to lower-level positions. The number of ministerial portfolios was increased to four, mostly in nonstrategic areas, and vice ministerial portfolios to six, including defense, home affairs, and information, thus partially meeting UNITA's demand for representation in these sectors. Six ambassadorial positions were also allocated to UNITA.

At the provincial level, the mediation team insisted that the number of governorships be increased to three, but the question was which ones. I recommended Huambo province because of its political and symbolic importance to UNITA, but my colleagues demurred, insisting this would be totally unacceptable to the government. As a compromise, we agreed to include the municipality of Huambo, which was equivalent geographically to a district of Huambo province. The three provinces selected were Lunda Sul, Cuando Cubango, and Uíge, each of which had a certain significance. Lunda Sul bordered Zaire, UNITA's ally in the northeast, located in the diamond-mining area; Cuando Cubango had provided a traditional safe haven to UNITA in the southeast, including its headquarters at Jamba; and Uíge was the strategic provincial town in the north that UNITA had captured in the postelection fighting. Five deputy governor positions were also agreed to, including Benguela, a coastal province south of Luanda that UNITA had won in the 1992 elections. Twenty municipalities, twenty-five vice municipalities, and forty-five communes were included.

After this deal had been worked out with the government delegation, it was presented to UNITA on March 10. Beye told the UNITA delegation that the mediation team had worked hard to produce this result and that the package was "reasonable." The observers also defended the proposals, pointing out that although the offer was not perfect, it was satisfactory and took into account UNITA's dual roles of being simultaneously part of the government and the major opposition party in the National Assembly.

Valentim responded that the proposals were seriously deficient, especially with respect to what was offered at the provincial and local levels. He pointed out that there was virtually no representation for UNITA in the provinces of Benguela, Bié, and Huambo, where UNITA had won overwhelming majorities in the 1992 elections. He also noted that the overall number of local positions was woefully inadequate: 3 out of 18 provinces, 20 out of 163 municipalities, and 45 out of 538 communes. Valentim questioned whether the government's offer really promoted a spirit of national reconciliation and ridiculed the government allegations that UNITA wanted to partition Angola. While Valentim appreciated the efforts of the mediation team, he concluded that more work needed to be done.

This put Beye and the observers into a bind. In my opinion, we had erred in accepting too quickly the government's offer without paying enough attention to UNITA's participation at the local level. This resulted in part from the parties' own preoccupations: UNITA's initial position paper had referred mainly to ministerial portfolios but had tended to gloss over representation at the local level. I blamed myself for not developing a better offer.

Faced with this impasse, Beye decided to go to Huambo to explain the March 10 proposals directly to Savimbi. Following his visit, he told the Troika that while the UNITA leader had a better appreciation of the state of the negotiations, Savimbi still insisted on the governorship of Huambo province. When the UNITA delegation returned to Lusaka a few days later and presented their counterproposals, these confirmed Beye's assessment. While there were a few quibbles here and there, UNITA basically accepted the numbers and positions identified at the national level. At the provincial level, Huambo and one deputy governorship had been added to the list, as well as a substantial increase in positions at the municipal level and below corresponding roughly to UNITA's vote tally in the 1992 elections.

MARCH 17 PROPOSALS

Beye was prepared to cut a new deal. Rocha-Paris and Botcharnikov were a bit more reserved because of the prior agreement with the government on the March 10 proposals. DeJarnette and I argued that the earlier offer needed to be improved if the impasse was to be broken. The key remained Huambo province. The team looked at various permutations before deciding that the number of provincial governors would remain unchanged at three, but two deputy governors would be added in Bié and Huambo provinces. With these changes, UNITA would at least be represented in the three provinces in which it had expressed strongest interest, as well as in the municipality of Huambo. At the local level, the mediation took the middle ground in allocating the number of positions to be offered at the municipal and communal levels. By and large, the mediators thought they had been judicious in making these admittedly somewhat arbitrary decisions.

Although the revised proposals tried to satisfy some of UNITA's concerns, they did not significantly restructure the March 10 proposals. The mediation team was surprised, therefore, when Higino categorically rejected the March 17 proposals, saying they were "unacceptable" and that the government's previous offer was "nonnegotiable." During our private conversations, DeJarnette and I told Muteka and Higino that the new proposals did not threaten the government, and were a small price to pay for peace. We also promised this was the final mediation position and that we would not ask for further changes. When Higino asked why we had backpedaled on the March 10 proposals, I replied we had acted too quickly without full information at our disposal. Besides, I said, *c'est la vie.* Looking disgruntled, Higino said the addition of the deputy governors for Bié and Huambo gave the government "heartburn."

Ever resourceful, Higino proposed what was called the "signing bonus option." If UNITA would accept the March 10 proposals, then a separate government-UNITA-U.S. agreement would be drawn up stating that UNITA would receive the positions described in the March 17 proposal at an agreed-on date after the signing of the peace accord. DeJarnette and I argued against that course of action, believing it would only muddy the waters further.

FIRST PRESIDENTIAL LETTER

The mediation had gone from one impasse to another. I decided the time had come to use one of the few arrows in my quiver—a presidential letter to Dos Santos. Fortunately, there was strong backup in Washington. At the National Security Council (NSC), Tony Lake, Nancy Soderburg, and Don Steinberg took a keen interest in Angola and the Lusaka peace talks. While the top levels of the State Department were not as engaged, George Moose and the Office of Southern African Affairs were. I telegraphed that we needed a letter now encouraging the government to accept the March 17 proposals and signaling that President Clinton looked forward to meeting with Dos Santos when a peace agreement was reached.

Washington reacted swiftly. In a letter dated March 25, 1994, President Clinton wrote to President Dos Santos:

> My Special Representative, Ambassador Paul Hare, informs me that the peace talks have reached a critical juncture on the issue of national reconciliation. The mediation has put a fair compromise package on the table, a package that recognizes the Government of Angola's unquestionable sovereignty yet provides UNITA an incentive to lay down its arms once and for all.
>
> Mr. President, I do not underestimate the difficulty of the decision before you. Your government won a free and fair election but was forced to fight for its very survival. Your commitment to peace, however, has enabled the international community to bring UNITA back to the

negotiating table. I ask that you lead the way toward peace by accepting the mediation's proposal. We will make every effort to persuade UNITA to follow your lead and accept this reasonable compromise.

It is my earnest hope, Mr. President, that we can meet soon after the accords are signed to discuss how we can work together to achieve peace and democracy in Angola.[5]

When the letter was shown to Maître Beye, he exclaimed that it was "a precious jewel." Initial reports from Luanda indicated that the letter had been "well received," buoying hopes that we were on the verge of a breakthrough.

The response several days later was disappointing. Dos Santos wrote that the government had been flexible and had made "substantial concessions" throughout the Lusaka talks, but there were limits to what it could concede.[6] While the president's letter would be taken into consideration, Dos Santos emphasized that the Angolan government alone would determine what was in its best interests. He also suggested that Angola and the United States should negotiate an "Agreement of Principles" to consolidate the peace process in Angola. A draft memorandum was attached that contained a laundry list of bilateral programs and guarantees that were akin to a NATO-like alliance.

Sensing Washington's disappointment at the response, the government realized it had overreached and sent a team to Lusaka to try to salvage something from the debris. I agreed to prepare a memorandum of conversation describing our present and future role in the peace process in order to provide reassurance of the American commitment. While professing to be satisfied with this gambit, the government still did not approve the March 17 package, which left the mediators back at square one.

Why did the Angolan government respond to President Clinton's letter in the way that it did? In part, someone had given bad advice, based on a total misreading of how Washington worked. Beyond its request for an all-encompassing relationship with the United States, however, the government's letter reflected deep suspicion of UNITA and the government's desire to be reassured that the United States would stand at its side if the peace talks collapsed and war resumed.

The letter created certain tensions within the Troika. Faced with the recalcitrant government position, the Portuguese and the Russians were increasingly inclined to revert to the March 10 proposals in the belief that the revised proposals were creating internal political difficulties in Luanda. Rocha-Paris was worried about the effect they were having on the stability of the government. I said the basic problem resulted from our original, too hasty agreement to the March 10 proposals. DeJarnette, who had not been in Lusaka during the earlier discussions, argued that the mediators had to stand firm. Beye concurred.

SECOND PRESIDENTIAL LETTER

In a further effort to obtain government agreement, Beye and I separately saw President Dos Santos in Luanda on April 11. Although I had been introduced to the president on an earlier occasion, this was my first substantive meeting with him. We met one-on-one, speaking in French. Dos Santos looked like the Hollywood casting of the ideal president, well dressed, handsome, his hair tinged with gray. He received me graciously and spoke in a softly modulated voice throughout the discussion. Behind the pleasant, mild-mannered demeanor, one sensed an iron resolve. It was easy to underestimate his strength.

As he had with Beye earlier in the day, Dos Santos explained the difficulties he was having internally in gaining support for the March 17 proposals. While he was prepared to take "any necessary risks" to achieve peace in Angola, he said he needed time and American cooperation to gain consensus for the new proposals within his constituency. True to form, he was playing his cards cautiously and avoiding making on-the-spot commitments. I explained the difficulties that the earlier letter had created in Washington and reiterated the importance of approving the mediation team's package to provide fresh impetus to the peace talks. At the end of the conversation, Dos Santos said, *"Je compte sur vous."* I replied that I too was counting on him. While we appeared to be at an impasse, I thought another nudge might be enough to get the government on board.

Presidential letters should be used sparingly and only for compelling reasons. After the fiasco of the earlier exchange, Washington contemplated whether another letter should be sent. Something, I thought, needed to be done. It was finally agreed that I should personally deliver a second presidential message to Dos Santos. The letter, dated April 23, 1994, was concise and to the point and was intended to convey the extent and seriousness of American engagement in the peace process:

> I was pleased to receive the report of my Special Representative, Ambassador Paul Hare, of his meeting with you April 11 and of your personal commitment to take the essential steps—as you said, "any necessary risks"—to achieve a peace agreement that would put an end to the suffering of the Angolan people.
>
> My government remains committed to finding a just and lasting peace for the Angolan people and is prepared in good faith to work together with you and your government to reach that objective as quickly as possible. . . . *I would also like to assure you that once a peace agreement is reached, the United States Government will be prepared to do all it can, within the United Nations and bilaterally, to ensure its successful implementation.* [Italics added]
>
> This cooperative effort will lay a solid foundation for our newly established bilateral relationship. I share the view expressed in your letter to me of March 28 that the development of that relationship is of mutual importance to our two governments and peoples.[7]

When I arrived in Luanda on April 29, I was told the president was out of the country and would be unable to see me until May 4 or 5. Generals N'dalu and Kopelipa suggested that the letter be delivered instead to the president of the National Assembly, the acting president. I declined, since I thought it was important to convey directly to President Dos Santos the mood of frustration that prevailed in Washington. I told the two generals that I would go to Lusaka and wait there until President Dos Santos was prepared to receive me. At the time, I thought the government was deliberately stalling while it conducted military offensives in the north. Indeed, soon after I left Luanda, N'dalatando, the capital of Cuanza Norte province, was captured by the FAA.

I finally saw President Dos Santos on May 6. After reading Clinton's letter, he said he would reply in about one week's time, following the inauguration of President Mandela of South Africa. Dos Santos again expressed doubt concerning UNITA's intentions and insisted that the South African political model, which had given significant positions to the opposition parties, could not be transplanted to Angolan soil. UNITA was, of course, comparing the two situations in order to improve its negotiating demands and put the government in an awkward position.

May was a frustrating month. Both parties hardened their positions and continued to pursue their military options. Beye and the Troika discussed what might be done if the talks continued to drift. Leaving Lusaka was ruled out, since it would be interpreted as an indication of international disinterest in the Angolan tragedy while the parties were still ostensibly prepared to negotiate. We also examined the possibility of reducing the UN and observer presence in Lusaka, including sending me home.

In mid-May, following discussions with Beye and Washington, we all agreed that I would go back to Washington for consultations. The Angolan government's delegation was informed there was little point in my remaining in Lusaka in view of the lack of progress in the talks. A few days later, Higino said President Dos Santos wanted to see me before I left Lusaka. On the evening of May 19, I arrived in Luanda on a government-provided jet, only to find no one at the airport except the political officer from the American embassy! She said some confusion had arisen about the meeting with the president, but that Generals N'dalu and Kopelipa were expected at the embassy that evening. When they arrived a couple of hours later, N'dalu explained apologetically that the president was tied up in a nonstop meeting with his political bureau and would not be available to meet with me. He indicated, however, that there would be a positive response to President Clinton in the next few days. I replied I hoped so, adding with a touch of exasperation that "the time had come to move, enough was enough!" I then went to Washington.

Other pressures were brought to bear on the government. Beye had delivered a letter to President Dos Santos from the UN secretary-general in support of the March 17 proposals; the Security Council was also scheduled to meet at the end of May to review the renewal of the UNAVEM II mandate. Since the government did not want to be criticized by the international community, the upcoming Security Council meeting served as an additional pressure. Indeed, just before the Security Council deadline, Dos Santos wrote to Clinton that his delegation in Lusaka had been instructed to consult with the mediation team in order to make "some minor changes to your suggestions and to provide a positive response."[8] The changes were minor and even increased the number of vice ministerial positions by one. Beye and the observers accepted the government's proposals in Lusaka on May 28. Subsequently, the "March 17 proposals" were referred to as the "May 28 proposals."

In a curious reading of our May 6 conversation, Dos Santos wrote in his letter to Clinton that I had made the interesting observation that the U.S. government would be ready to provide assistance to the Angolan armed forces so that they could respond to any violations of the peace agreement that he hoped would be reached in Lusaka. I did not recall making such a sweeping commitment. Nor did DeJarnette. The comment demonstrated how determined the government was to avoid a repetition of what had happened during the Bicesse period.

THE PROCESS OF GETTING UNITA ABOARD

It had taken almost ten weeks to obtain the government's approval of the May 28 proposals. Although UNITA knew that the mediators were working on a revised offer, we had not specifically informed the party of what it might contain. On May 28, the mediation team gave the revised proposals to UNITA. Ten days later, UNITA provided its response, accepting the revised numbers and positions but requesting that Huambo be added to the list of provincial governorships.

We were once again at an impasse, even though the gap between the two sides had been significantly reduced. While there had been a faint hope that UNITA might accept the proposals just as they were, its response was not unanticipated. In Lusaka and Washington, various options had been considered for responding to this contingency. As a first step, it was decided I would return to Lusaka, this time carrying a letter from President Clinton to Savimbi, which was to be delivered in person.

When I returned to Lusaka, Beye and my Troika colleagues decided that the whole team should go to Huambo in order to present a unified front. On June 18, we flew to Huambo, where we were greeted by the UNITA provincial governor, no doubt present to underline that we were now in UNITA territory and that the governorship of the province was rightfully UNITA's. The reception was well organized and in the African tradition. Banners proclaimed in French, presumably for the benefit of Beye, that the 1992 elections had been a fraud, along with other UNITA slogans. Traditional dancers gyrated in circles to the insistent rhythmic beat of drums, while a crowd of well-wishers looked on curiously as the resplendently robed, smiling Maître Beye, trailed by three white diplomats, entered the shell-pocked terminal building.

On the drive into town, we saw the destruction of war everywhere. No building had been left untouched by the fighting. Huambo looked like downtown Beirut at the height of the civil war. Rocha-Paris was shocked, remembering the city from its better days during the Bicesse period. When the convoy eventually arrived downtown, another large crowd had assembled and was shouting greetings and slogans calling for peace in Angola. The occasion seemed almost festive.

Once inside, we mingled with the UNITA officials and military commanders while waiting for Savimbi to arrive. You had the distinct sense that this group had lived and fought together for a long time in a common cause. They had the esprit de corps of comrades-at-arms, or so it seemed to me.

During the first session, Beye and the three observers met with Savimbi and a few of his colleagues in a small, dingy room upstairs. The nonstop, orchestrated chants of the crowd reverberated loudly inside the room, making it difficult to hear what was being said. Was this a deliberate ploy to rattle us or simply a demonstration of UNITA's ability to mobilize the masses? It was hard to tell. The noise did not seem to bother General Ben Ben, who was sitting next to me: midway through the meeting, I heard the clack of a pen hitting the floor, and I turned to find the general fast asleep!

After the customary welcomes, Beye explained the rationale behind the May 28 proposals and how the mediation team had tried to take into consideration UNITA's concerns by offering the party the deputy governorship of Huambo province and the position of administrator of Huambo municipality. He also asked what thoughts Savimbi might have on his future role in the government, which many felt was the key to reaching a peace agreement. The observers supported Beye's arguments and asserted the urgent need to conclude the negotiations quickly so that the fighting in Angola could be stopped.

Savimbi listened attentively throughout the presentations. He said that the May 28 proposals were a good basis on which to proceed—in fact, "90 percent" of the work had been done, the only remaining problem being Huambo province. He dismissed the question of what his status might be, saying he was not the one who would make the offer. While emphasizing his total commitment to peace, he castigated the government for carrying out military offensives, including air attacks against Huambo city. In short, Savimbi indicated that UNITA's position remained unchanged.

Following the general meeting, Beye and each observer met separately with Savimbi. This was my first meeting with the UNITA leader, although I had spoken with Savimbi on the phone in February when there had been a serious escalation of hostilities, and tensions were running high. At that time, I had noted Savimbi was "clear, cogent, and nonemotional." He was the same on this occasion, at ease, projecting confidence and control. He welcomed me warmly, saying he had hoped to meet me for some time. We spoke in English.

I told Savimbi that we had at long last the opportunity to end the Angolan tragedy, which was why I had come with a letter from President Clinton. The letter read in part:

> Ambassador Hare informs me that the Government of Angola has accepted the revised package presented by the mediation on national reconciliation. We believe that this package also meets UNITA's political concerns. Although I understand that the UNITA delegation in Lusaka has expressed some reservations about the mediation proposal, I ask that you display the wisdom and political courage to choose peace by accepting the proposed package on national reconciliation.
>
> UNITA now has a momentous and historic opportunity: after more than seven months of difficult negotiations, an agreement is within reach. I recognize and applaud the important role you have played in

bringing the peace process this far. With the fruits of our efforts so close, your leadership is more important than ever.

The new dawn of democracy in South Africa came because the leaders of South Africa had the courage to cooperate and compromise. I look to you to take similar steps for peace and to end Angola's long and tragic night.[9]

Savimbi pronounced it was a "good letter" and gave it to Valentim, who held it almost reverentially in his hands. The UNITA leader said he appreciated American involvement in the peace process, which was essential as he had indicated in a letter to President Clinton the previous month. However, Huambo province remained important. Indeed, it was indispensable, as it was UNITA's regional base. I replied that while I understood his concerns, he should also understand ours, that we had worked hard to get the government to accept the mediation proposals and that we could not demand more: "The president's letter made a final statement of where we stood. An issue of even greater importance was *who occupied* the post of governor. Perhaps that is what we should be looking at." We parted amicably, promising to stay in touch.

Before leaving, the entire entourage assembled on the balcony overlooking the crowd that had continued chanting and singing with remarkable stamina throughout the day. When Beye appeared next to Savimbi, they shouted out his name repeatedly in deafening unison: "Beye, Beye, Beye." I turned to Manuvakola and said I had just figured out who should govern Huambo! He smiled.

THE SOUTH AFRICAN CARD

We had failed to reach agreement in Huambo. What were we to do next? Beye and the observers had already thought about this, knowing that it was unlikely the Huambo visit would produce a breakthrough. We concluded the best option would be to engage Nelson Mandela. With his unquestionable political and moral stature on the international scene, the South African president just might be able to persuade Savimbi to accept the mediation proposals.

This was not our first talk with the new leaders of South Africa. I had met Thabo Mbeki, South Africa's first vice president and a colleague from my earlier assignment to Zambia, in New York at the end of May to brief him on the negotiations. Despite the enormous challenges facing the government at home, South Africa remained keenly interested in Angola. I had told Mbeki at that time that the Lusaka peace process was the only game in town and that South Africa could best assist the process by maintaining lines of communication to both sides. Mbeki had a sophisticated understanding of the Angolan situation and wanted to be kept informed.

Through the efforts of Princeton Lyman, the American ambassador in South Africa, the trip was quickly arranged. The mediation team flew to Cape Town on June 23 and, before seeing Mandela, sketched out the game plan to Derek Auret, an old hand on Africa at the Foreign Ministry. We explained that although the talks had come to an impasse over who would govern Huambo province, it still might be possible to reach an understanding on how the governor would be selected that would take into account UNITA sensitivities. It was also important to get a better understanding of what role Savimbi might play in a future government. We thought Mandela could usefully explore these issues if he was prepared to invite the UNITA leader to South Africa. Other confidence-building measures were discussed. Although peacekeepers were ruled out, South Africa might be able to provide other types of assistance to support the peace process. This could give UNITA additional reassurance that it would not be abandoned once an agreement was reached.[10]

Mandela was extraordinary—warm, understanding, gracious. For example, when the tea tray was brought in by a young white girl, her voice was a mere whisper when she asked what Mandela would like to drink. Since Mandela is hard of hearing, this led to several moments of awkward silence before an aide intervened, the girl tongue-tied, the president puzzled but smiling.

During the substantive part of the session, Mandela said he wanted to do everything he could to help the peace process in Angola. He was prepared to invite Savimbi to South Africa, but he did not want to create problems with Morocco and the Ivory Coast, since the three countries had agreed in 1993 to a joint plan for bringing Dos Santos and Savimbi together to end the Angolan conflict. Beye assured Mandela that those two governments would be informed he was undertaking this initiative at the request of the United Nations and observer states. So far, the meeting had gone well.

On leaving the meeting, an aide told Mandela that the press was waiting in the next room. This was totally unexpected. If the participants had known that a press conference had been arranged, the normal procedure would have been to agree in advance on what would be said. In the event, Mandela readily agreed to meet with the press and then proceeded to give full details of what had been discussed, including his intention to invite Savimbi to South Africa. Since the Angolan government had not been informed of these plans, this created an immediate problem. South Africa's deputy foreign minister, Aziz Pahad, leaned over and whispered in my ear that he hoped they had not just blown the initiative. I chalked the experience up to the teething problems of a new government.

On my return to Lusaka, I met with the UNITA delegation prior to going back to Washington. I said I had come back to the region to deliver the presidential letter to Savimbi and participate in the meeting with Mandela. I urged again that UNITA accept the mediation package without delay, adding that while I knew UNITA felt the mediators had painted themselves into a corner, there was simply no feasible alternative to the Lusaka process. Valentim talked about escaping from the legalisms of the present approach and trying something new. I gathered that what he meant was that UNITA wanted to break out of the Lusaka process.

The situation did not look promising. The negotiations were hung up over Huambo, while the fighting intensified inside Angola. The secretary-general reported to the Security Council that the security situation had deteriorated rapidly in June, which had led to a countrywide suspension of humanitarian aid.[11] The government was concentrating its efforts on establishing a dominant position in the northern region, while UNITA was trying to consolidate its position in the southwestern and central regions. Prior to the Security Council meeting at the end of June, I sent the following assessment to Washington:

> Equally important is a harsh condemnation of the military escalation within Angola and a clarion call for an immediate cessation of hostilities throughout the country. This will not please the government which wants to freeze the situation around Malange and Kuito, while

continuing their offensives in the north and elsewhere. The government should not be allowed to have it both ways. While both sides share culpability for the renewed fighting, the government, in my opinion, bears the main responsibility for the disaster we are witnessing when they unleashed their "super offensive" in the north several months ago.[12]

Against the backdrop of escalating warfare, the Security Council called for restraint but declared its readiness to impose additional sanctions against UNITA if the May 28 proposals were not accepted by the end of July.[13] Meanwhile, at Beye's initiative, the Zambians also got involved. President Frederick Chiluba had a meeting with Dos Santos in Luanda on July 5, during which the Angolan president made it clear, referring to Huambo, that he was not prepared to give away what had been seized by force of arms. The next day, a Zambian team, led by Vernon Mwaanga, chairman of the parliamentary commission for foreign affairs, and Enoch Kavindele, a businessman, saw Savimbi in Huambo. What transpired was not entirely clear. The Zambians insisted they had not deviated from the mediation team's proposals, though they had discussed what role Savimbi might have in the government, such as being a vice president. Other reports suggested that the possibility of appointing a "neutral governor" for Huambo or offering UNITA an additional governorship had also been raised. The mediation team spent a lot of time refuting the notion that there was a separate Zambian initiative. In retrospect, the Zambian intervention created more problems than it resolved.

THE GATHERING CLOUDS

During this impasse in the negotiations, the mediation team came under increasing criticism. On the evening of June 21, Beye, visibly upset, had come to my hotel room. He said he had received several telephone calls from New York saying that the Americans thought he was too pro-government. I said I was astonished by this information, since it contradicted everything I had said about his leadership of the negotiations. Undoubtedly, the impression that Beye was pro-government arose from our position on the Huambo question. Some thought UNITA had a legitimate claim to Huambo, and while they had a point, this view did not take into account the fact that Huambo had been captured following a fifty-five-day siege, nor did it acknowledge the difficult path that had finally arrived at the May 28 proposals. I told Beye that I considered any attack on himself to be equally directed at me, and added that if Washington tried to change the package, I would resign my position.

UNITA took every opportunity to demonstrate that the mediation team was biased. The Free Angola Information Service in Washington (the UNITA lobbying office) released a news bulletin in July, quoting Shawn McCormick, the deputy director of African studies at the Center for Strategic and International Studies, in which he purportedly said that Portugal, Russia, and the United States were wrong not to have given UNITA the governorship of Huambo: "If Lusaka was intended to be a process of national reconciliation and its function is to heal the wounds from Bicesse, then UNITA should have what it legitimately won at the ballot box."[14] Gerald Bender, an internationally recognized expert on Angola, said it was imperative to expand the package by adding either Huambo or Bié; otherwise, he was certain UNITA would not accept the proposals.[15] Other authorities inside the administration shared these views.

During July and August, the South African gambit continued to be played out. UNITA sent an advance team to South Africa in July to prepare the agenda for Savimbi's visit and flatly told the South Africans that the UN-led effort was fatally flawed. UNITA's Political Commission subsequently issued a communiqué on July 27 stating that the meeting with President Mandela remained "extremely important," presumably to ward off further sanctions by the Security Council, scheduled to meet at the end of the month.[16] At the request of the Americans and South Africans, the Security Council postponed a decision on imposing additional sanctions on UNITA in order to give more time to arrange a meeting between Mandela and Savimbi.[17] After further consultations in South Africa during August, UNITA must have concluded that the South Africans would not set up a negotiating track apart from the UN-led effort and that there was little point in having Savimbi meet with Mandela. The trip never happened.

As the countdown continued to the August deadline and the prospect of new sanctions, UNITA began to shift gears. On August 20,

Savimbi sent a message to President Chiluba in which he renounced UNITA's claim to the governorship of Huambo province. This was subsequently confirmed in a letter, dated August 30, from Manuva-kola to Beye. Later that same day, Beye sent a letter to UNITA and the government, which indicated that in his opinion UNITA had formally accepted the May 28 proposals. Now the government balked. It claimed the exchange of letters did not constitute formal acceptance of the plan, especially citing that part of the letter in which UNITA asserted it reserved the right to approve the nominee for governor of Huambo. Dos Santos publicly declared that this qualification was unacceptable. The government stepped up its pressure. In New York, it pressed for additional sanctions against UNITA; in Angola, the air force attacked Huambo on August 31, interrupting the talks for five days. Despite adverse publicity, these tactics seemed to have an effect. On September 5, UNITA sent a follow-up letter unequivocally accepting the May 28 proposals. On this somewhat bittersweet note, the six-month saga ended.[18]

SOME OBSERVATIONS

Throughout the six months of negotiations on national reconciliation issues in Lusaka, the fighting inside Angola had ebbed and flowed but had progressively shifted in the government's favor. A combination of factors accounted for this change, including the government's massive arms purchases, recruitment of mercenaries, and buildup of its army. In mid-July, the FAA captured the town of Cafunfo, located in the diamond-rich region of the Lundas, while also advancing toward Uíge and Negage, and other UNITA positions in the northern region. In the central highlands, the government had held Kuito/Bié despite the great odds (the city was pulverized in the process) and had increased its pressure on Huambo city. The changing balance of forces directly impacted on the pace and substance of the negotiations. While UNITA had dawdled during the first phase of the talks, the government now slowed the pace in order to give its forces time to seize additional ground and provincial towns. Aside from rhetorical denunciations, the international community could do little to stop the fighting.

In their respective negotiating tactics, each side tried to show it had the upper hand. Huambo became the centerpiece of this test of wills, assuming a larger-than-life significance. From a practical point of view, the government could have given up the governorship of Huambo without any harm to its real interests, and so could have UNITA. But Huambo was a symbol reflecting the relative strengths of the two parties. The government wanted to demonstrate its dominance (and legitimacy), while UNITA wished to retain its separate power base and identity. The parties knew each other well—perhaps too well. While their maneuvers could be frustrating to the mediators, they had their own logic.

Although the pace and content of the negotiations were determined predominately by the dynamics of the battlefield, the voice of the international community demanding an end to the bloodshed helped to shape the environment and to influence the outcome. Neither side wanted to be censured or sanctioned by the Security Council. The government accepted the mediation proposals just before the May Security Council meeting; UNITA did the same at the end of August.

While the Troika vessel sprang some leaks, it did not sink, largely because Beye did not waver in his support of the May 28 proposals. Later, Washington's continued backing of the proposals, despite mounting criticisms from UNITA and other observers, was decisive. If Washington had tried to tinker with the package (and some policymakers were tempted to do so), it would have completely unraveled what had been achieved in the negotiations and been contrary to the positions that President Clinton had taken in his letters to Dos Santos and Savimbi.

Although attention was focused on the national reconciliation package during this six-month period, the negotiators discussed a host of other issues. Two were especially important. One section of the protocol dealt with the conclusion of the electoral process. Since Dos Santos had not received a majority in the September 1992 elections, the constitution required a runoff. In Lusaka the parties agreed that the second round of presidential elections would be deferred until the UN special representative had determined that the conditions on the ground would permit a free and fair vote. The negotiators did not want to repeat the Bicesse experience, when elections had been held before the military and other parts of the agreement had been satisfactorily implemented. It was also understood that a transitional period of at least several years was needed to mend the wounds of civil war.

Another section of the protocol addressed the role of the United Nations and the observer states. Unlike Bicesse, the UN special representative was given real authority and powers, most importantly by chairing the Joint Commission, the body established to oversee the implementation of the protocol in which the government, UNITA, and observer delegations were represented. While these attributions undercut to some extent Angolan sovereignty, they were essential if real muscle was to be put into the implementation process. On several occasions, I jokingly told Beye that he was going to be more powerful than the president. While this was not true, President Dos Santos sometimes ruefully commented along similar lines.

The almost nonstop negotiations in Lusaka had been protracted. Could the mediators have done anything to speed up the process? We might have pressed the government harder to offer additional provincial governor positions, though it is doubtful if it would have ever yielded in offering Huambo or Bié provinces to UNITA. Since Huambo was UNITA's bottom line, I doubt that alternative proposals would have produced a different or quicker result.

From this trap there was no easy escape. The mediators did their best to develop reasonable proposals, and then they stuck to them. Sometimes this is the best (and only) course to take.

5

The Start of Implementation

With the Huambo issue at last resolved, the negotiators had conquered the biggest stumbling block. Nevertheless, the talks continued for seven more weeks on issues of secondary importance, such as what name would be given to the body that would supervise the implementation of the peace accords. Deciding which specific municipalities and communes would be given to UNITA led to further haggling. By October 17, the last substantive issues were resolved, leaving only the timetable to be discussed. After consulting with and getting the go-ahead from the leadership of each side in Luanda and Huambo, the heads of the delegations and Beye initialed the Lusaka Protocol on October 31, just before the Security Council was to meet. The formal signing was scheduled to take place two weeks later, on November 15, at Mulungushi Hall.

The talks during September and October were slowed, as before, by developments on the battlefield. In his report to the Security Council of October 20, the secretary-general reported:

> My Special Representative, supported by the representatives of the observer states, has on numerous occasions urged the Government and UNITA to refrain from conducting offensive military operations which not only continue to destroy human lives and property but also threaten the successful conclusion of the Lusaka peace talks. Regrettably, their admonitions have been heeded only to a limited extent, especially in recent days.[1]

The report chronicled the extent of the fighting, especially in the northern and central regions of the country. The government's offensives in the north targeted the oil town of Soyo (twice taken by UNITA), located on the coast just south of Cabinda, and Uíge and Negage, the latter being the site of the most important airfield in the northern region. UNITA was just trying to hold on or engage in diversionary military maneuvers. As the fighting intensified, the war of words became more bellicose. The general staff of the Angolan Armed Forces issued a communiqué on September 19 detailing what it described as an "unprecedented increase" in offensive military operations by UNITA throughout Angola.[2] This provided the smoke screen behind which the government could claim its forces were only reacting to UNITA military actions. At the same time, the president's spokesman, Alderniro da Conceicao, indicated that he did not expect the talks to conclude quickly—a statement presumably intended to give the FAA more time to carry out its offensives.[3]

In response to this increased military activity, UNITA threw down the gauntlet, declaring that the government's offensives could derail the peace process. Lukamba Paulo "Gato" warned that the government's offensives against Soyo and Huambo could undermine what had been accomplished in the peace talks in Lusaka. UNITA's radio station, the Voice of Resistance of the Black Cockerel, stated that UNITA's military forces (FALA) in the Soyo region had been put on alert because "of the arrival in Luanda of Texaco magnates who are willing to invest in Soyo at the cost of blood." The commentary concluded that "the FALA Command, however, assures that no oil will leave Soyo to finance the unjust war that José Eduardo Dos Santos' organization is waging against the Angolan people."[4] The broadcast conspicuously omitted the fact that UNITA had destroyed the oil facility at the cost of millions of dollars.

THE FALL OF HUAMBO

When the Lusaka Protocol was initialed, the mediation team assumed that the fighting would diminish, even though according to the agreement, a formal cease-fire would not go into effect until two days after the official signing of the protocol. Repeated government assurances given privately and publicly that the FAA did not intend to capture Huambo or otherwise engage in offensive operations reinforced the mediators' assumption. Just after the protocol was initialed, the FAA spokesman, Brigadier José Manuel Jota, told the government-controlled newspaper *Jornal de Angola* that the army did not intend to take Huambo.[5] As the offensive continued, Brigadier Jota changed his tune. Six days later, in talking about the army's occupation of the governmental palace in Huambo on November 7, Jota explained:

> We have a country at war. The war has not ended. The war will only end with a cease-fire. Naturally we have to take some initiatives because UNITA did not stop waging war. UNITA continued to attack, and if it has the opportunity to take a municipality it will, until the date of the cease-fire. We cannot remain sitting on our hands. The government's troop movements are not unlawful, they are not violating anything.[6]

The government's seizure of Huambo was condemned by the Security Council and the U.S. government.[7] In a communiqué issued by the president's office of UNITA on November 8, Savimbi expressed his profound gratitude for the positions taken by the United Nations and the United States and claimed that the MPLA was conducting inhuman genocide with the assistance of mercenaries from South Africa to as far away as Brazil.[8] The government, meanwhile, was stung by the American criticism. Reflecting an instinctive distrust of American intentions, the secretary of state for cooperation, Johny Eduardo Pinock, asked why the United States had not made a similar condemnation when UNITA occupied Huambo in 1993.[9]

Neither international condemnation nor UNITA's defiant declarations that it would never give up its birthright Huambo prevailed. Some had thought UNITA would be able to defend the city at least until the signing of the protocol and the enactment of a cease-fire two days later. But the city fell rather quickly. Why? Were the government's army and air force too strong? Had the mercenaries played a decisive role, as UNITA claimed? Or was UNITA's military arm weaker than expected? All of these factors contributed to the fall of Huambo, but it is difficult to single out which one was decisive, partly because it is hard to obtain reliable information about

Angolan developments. According to some government representatives, the FAA had not intended to capture Huambo, but when
UNITA's defenses evaporated, the army filled the vacuum. The only
problem with this interpretation is that the government, following
the fall of Huambo, continued to conduct its offensives in the north
against Uíge and M'banza Congo, as well as against Cuito Cuanavale
in the south. Clearly, its objective was to capture all provincial capitals before the peace treaty was signed. And except for M'banza
Congo, it succeeded.

THE TRUCE OFFER

According to the Lusaka timetable, high-level military talks were to
be held in Lusaka ten days after the initialing of the protocol to discuss various technical issues relating to the cease-fire and security
arrangements for Savimbi and other senior UNITA officials. The fighting inside Angola upset this timetable. Although the government
sent its military delegation to Lusaka, UNITA's military representatives did not come, which raised the very real question of whether
UNITA intended to go through with the signing of the protocol.

When I returned to Lusaka on November 9, coinciding with the
fall of Huambo, there was deep gloom about what the future might
hold. Rocha-Paris was upset by the government's military offensives
following the initialing of the Lusaka Protocol, as he felt these actions
contradicted assurances previously made. Beye was doing everything he could to salvage the peace process. In my discussions with
the government delegation, I expressed my personal dismay at what
had transpired since I had left Lusaka in late October and stated that
at a minimum the government's military offensives had to stop immediately. With the UNITA delegation, I pointed out our condemnation of the government's actions but added that no reasonable alternative existed to the peace accords. I also said that either George
Moose, who was coming to Lusaka for the signing of the protocol, or
I—or both of us—would be prepared to accompany Savimbi from
wherever he might be to Lusaka in order to ensure his personal
security. Beye made a similar offer.

With the peace agreement hanging by a thread, Beye and the observers insisted that the government had to demonstrate that it was prepared to call a halt to the fighting. The international outcry had an effect. On November 13, the Angolan government issued a declaration stating its willingness to establish a nationwide truce.[10] The UNITA military team arrived in Lusaka the next day. Later on November 14, UNAVEM issued a public communiqué stating that following meetings with the government, UNITA, and the observer states, it was agreed that the Lusaka Protocol would be signed on November 20 by President Dos Santos and Dr. Savimbi. Furthermore, the parties would work on a priority basis to set a date and hour for establishing a nationwide truce.[11]

The only problem with this revised timetable was that a number of African heads of state, including Mandela (South Africa) and Mugabe (Zimbabwe), had already arrived in the Zambian capital in anticipation of the November 15 signing ceremony. They were a disgruntled lot. According to one report, Mugabe was especially upset that the government had persisted on the path of war when peace seemed so near. Since Mugabe was identified with the Angolan government, at least in the eyes of UNITA, his message had special resonance.

The military group concluded the truce agreement on November 15. The nationwide truce was to take effect twenty-four hours later, specifically at 8.00 P.M. (local time) on November 16, in order to give enough time for the orders to be transmitted by the respective military commands. Hope sprang up that the peace agreement had been salvaged. But as had happened too many times before, the truce went up in smoke almost as soon as it was signed. UNITA reported that the FAA captured the provincial capital of Uíge in the early morning of November 17, just hours after the truce had begun.[12] Although the government claimed their forces had taken Uíge before the truce,[13] this conflicted with information received from independent observers in Uíge. The mediators had a sense of déjà vu. Because the "climate of war" persisted in Angola, Manuvakola announced that UNITA was suspending its participation in the military talks, and he would await further instructions from his headquarters about whether to stay in Lusaka or to leave.[14]

With the peace agreement looking increasingly shaky, I met with Manuvakola. He could be tough and combative, but he was also intelligent and a person of integrity—though I have to admit, when he used elliptical Ovimbundu folktales involving different species of local animals to illuminate his line of reasoning, I would get completely lost. Now, Manuvakola appeared tired; he seemed to be carrying a heavy weight on his shoulders. When I asked if UNITA would choose war or peace, he replied he was still waiting to hear from his leaders, but because of the unsettled security situation, communications were difficult. I said I understood the difficulties in which UNITA found itself but still believed the only option was to go ahead with the signing of the Lusaka Protocol. Did UNITA really have a choice? Manuvakola said there was an alternative. UNITA could go back to the bush and conduct a guerrilla war. Over time, the situation would change, as it had in the past. This corresponded to what he had said publicly in an interview with the BBC:

> If the government wants to follow the military option, we seriously need to think about a military option, as well. I would like to say that, so far, we have been waging a conventional war to defend cities and towns, which is not our specialty. Our specialty is bush war. That is our war. We think we are not on a path of weakness, but a path of strength. We can adapt ourselves to the new situation quickly, and we will see whether Angola will have peace or war for a few more years.[15]

THE SIGNING OF THE LUSAKA PROTOCOL

In the end, UNITA decided to sign the Lusaka Protocol. Citing security considerations, Savimbi did not come to Lusaka, despite entreaties from Beye and the United States; instead, he designated Manuvakola to sign on behalf of the party. Even though the peace agreement had been saved, this was not the way it should have been. A whiff of disappointment hung in the air. As various dignitaries arrived at the airport to attend the signing ceremony, the Zambian cabinet had gathered to welcome them. When President Dos Santos's imminent arrival was announced, one minister shouted out, "We want Savimbi!" His colleagues laughed and applauded. While the comment was said humorously, it reflected a commonly held view that Savimbi represented an authentic strain of African identity and nationalism, and that something important was missing on that day.

The signing ceremony at Mulungushi Hall was solemn, filled with appropriately worded statements of peace and the rites of protocol. Manuvakola's invocation was moving:

> The war's consequences have been heavy. I would agree that we have in Angola one million dead, one hundred thousand crippled, five million displaced people, two million refugees in neighboring countries, a debt exceeding $20 billion, and three million starving Angolans. Those numbers are not far from the truth. Our beautiful country is dying. Angola needs several decades of peace to rid itself of ruins. Let the sight of rubble be forever present before the leaders' eyes so that the flame of peace will light constructive solutions in their minds.

He concluded on this dramatic note: "On behalf of President Savimbi, I give UNITA's hand to the government of the Republic of Angola for the sake of peace and national reconciliation."[16] With that, he shook hands with the Angolan foreign minister, Venâncio de Moura, who had signed the protocol on behalf of the government, and embraced President Dos Santos. It was a sweet moment.

RETURN TO REALITY

Following the declaration of the cease-fire on November 22, the fighting began to subside, though both sides accused the other of initiating military attacks. For UNAVEM, the most urgent requirement was to get its military observers into the countryside to monitor the cease-fire. As had been evident throughout the negotiations, unless a neutral third party was present on the ground, it would not be possible to investigate cease-fire violations. At the end of November, Beye decided to deploy the eighty military and police observers already in the country to more sensitive locations. As a first step, UNAVEM regional headquarters were established in Huambo, Luena, Menongue, Saurimo, and Uíge, in addition to the existing headquarters in Lubango. But much more had to be done.

The Security Council had already foreseen the necessity of dispatching additional observers if a cease-fire were declared. Security Council Resolution 952 (October 27) authorized the restoration of

UNAVEM II to its previous levels of 350 military observers and 126 police observers, but it inserted a caveat. The deployment would be contingent on an "effective cease-fire" being in place. Although it was understandable that members of the Security Council did not want to place unarmed observers in harm's way, this qualification jeopardized the possibility of ever attaining "an effective cease-fire." On the recommendation of his special representative, supported by the observer countries, the secretary-general bit the bullet when he informed the council on December 7 that the cease-fire was "generally holding, despite some initial difficulties" and that both the government and UNITA wanted UN observers to be deployed as soon as possible.[17] On that basis, he had decided to go ahead with the planned enlargement.

The second imperative was to commence the work of the Joint Commission, the body responsible for supervising the implementation of the agreement. Getting the UNITA representatives to Luanda was not easy. Although the first meeting of the Joint Commission in Luanda was scheduled for November 29, UNITA's representatives did not arrive in the Angolan capital until December 4. According to Beye, President Mobutu of Zaire was instrumental in persuading UNITA to send its delegates to Luanda.

The first session of the Joint Commission was held on December 4, just hours after the arrival of the UNITA delegation. It was an important—indeed, critical—benchmark in the peace process. In his opening statement, Beye declared that this moment was a victory over "the enemies of peace," who otherwise went unidentified. The prime minister of Angola, Marcolino Moco, expressed his conviction that "this house—which will host the Joint Commission—will never be the stage for sad scenes for our people, like those that [were] experienced before the conflict erupted and that we are now trying to bring under control with the Lusaka Protocol." Isaias Samakuva, the UNITA representative, said:

> We are back in Luanda today, two years after our dramatic exit from this city. I do not wish to rehash the sad events that marked our departure from Luanda in 1992, but if our real desire is to build solid foundations for a better future for our people and country, then each one of us—whether he or she is a political leader or a common citizen—

must use the past as a reference so that we can correct the errors each and every one of us has made.[18]

Samakuva added that although the negotiations had been long and difficult, the implementation of the agreement would be even more difficult. How true this prediction would prove to be!

ROCKY MOMENTS

December was a difficult month. On December 7, the U.S. Department of State issued a press release that welcomed the UNITA delegation to Luanda but also expressed concern about the continued presence of mercenaries in Angola, specifically referring to Executive Outcomes, a South African firm that had a contract with the Angolan government.[19] The press release, issued primarily in response to congressional concerns, was not relevant to the needs of Angola at that time. The Angolan government responded angrily two days later, stating that "unless there is a deliberate intention to create an additional embarrassment to the Angolan government," this issue should have been dealt with bilaterally.[20] The question of mercenaries would remain a thorn in the side of the peace process.

In the middle of the month, UNITA raised alarm bells over continuing government offensives throughout the country, backed by "mercenaries from all backgrounds and other criminals."[21] A communiqué issued by UNITA's Political Commission on December 14 declared, "The MPLA wants to transform Angola into Africa's Bosnia."[22] Lukamba Paulo Gato echoed these points in an interview with the BBC and also complained about the lack of attention that Angola was receiving from the international community. He argued that the FAA would occupy all of the districts and communes of Angola before the peacekeepers ever arrived—the Blue Helmets' arrival was now expected to be voted on in the Security Council on February 8, 1995.[23] What was the point? he asked rhetorically. Later, Savimbi had some pithy comments on the projected late arrival of the Blue Helmets.

The process is so flawed that even at the point of its conception [Lusaka Protocol] no account was taken of the fact that there was a war going on here. And if there was a war going on, you should not leave the two sides alone from 20 November to 8 February 1995. What are people to do for all of that time? Stare at one another like dummies?[24]

In Luanda, the usually unflappable UNITA representative, Isaias Samakuva, did not rule out the possibility that guerrilla warfare might resume.

Most disturbing was an interview given by Savimbi sometime in December 1994 to the French publication *Libération,* his first public commentary in many months. Undoubtedly fueled by the government's propaganda machine, rumors had previously circulated that Savimbi had been wounded or killed, operated on in Morocco, or removed by a palace coup d'état. Although his statements were couched in ambiguity, Savimbi communicated his fear that the peace process could be derailed by the so-called government offensives. He categorically ruled out going to Luanda to meet with President Dos Santos, saying, "I am not crazy! Why get myself killed?" Striking at the heart of the Lusaka Protocol, Savimbi said his troops were not prepared to be billeted under the present circumstances. He also chastised Maître Beye:

> As for Mr. Beye, he disappointed me. It was not his place to say that I did not come to Lusaka for the signature of the agreement on 20 November because I was "a beaten man" or because I did not want to be "humiliated." He talks too much! Now he wants to come here to meet with me. It is no longer worth the trouble. It is over. I do not want to talk to him any longer.
>
> [REPORTER:] You no longer want to see the UN special representative, you do not want to go to Luanda, and your troops refuse to be billeted. Do you not get the impression that there is a problem?
>
> [SAVIMBI:] Of course there is a problem, and I am frank enough not to hide it. UNITA is experiencing its deepest crisis since it was created 28 years ago.[25]

Presidential spokesman da Conceicao said Savimbi's statements showed UNITA's lack of will in complying with the Lusaka Protocol, which he described as being in a "precarious situation."[26] The minister of justice (a former UNITA member), Paulo Tchipilika, commented: "It is a pity, because Dr. Savimbi's remarks allow us unequivocally to conclude that he is still very poorly advised. He appears not to have grasped yet that we are a mere five years away from the 21st century."[27]

On a more positive note, Savimbi declared in an end-of-the-year interview that he would receive Maître Beye, saying, "He can come. . . . He spoke badly. But he is an official, not a politician, so that the matter can be ignored."[28] However, his overall tone continued to be somber, even truculent, casting large doubts over the Lusaka Protocol, the role of the United Nations, and the prospects for peace in Angola. It was not a good way to begin the new year. In contrast, President Dos Santos took a more Olympian tone in his New Year's message to the nation:

> It is clear Angola's peace process will not be easy. That is why each of us should make an extra effort to overcome eventual contradictions and adopt in our daily life an open, tolerant, and cooperative attitude. It is necessary to create the most profound solidarity by looking at every other citizen as a brother and member of the Angolan family.[29]

STABILIZATION OF THE CEASE-FIRE

When I went to Angola at the beginning of January 1995, the situation was fragile. In an initial evaluation, I informed Washington:

> The government seems confident, though concerned by Dr. Savimbi's public posture, which casts doubt on the peace process. UNITA is wary and feels victimized. They are still smarting from the seizure of Huambo, following the initialing of the Lusaka Protocol and the failure of the international community and the mediation to stop the government's offensives. This adds massively to their sense of distrust and insecurity about the future.[30]

The immediate challenge was to consolidate the cease-fire by deploying the UN observers to the field. Although UNAVEM worked hard to get the teams into the field, the pace was slow. One problem concerned access to UNITA-controlled areas, especially in the Uíge and Negage region. Another was associated with the shortage of vehicles, generators, and other basic items needed to equip the team sites. UNAVEM also lacked adequate air transport, especially helicopter support to fly to remote areas. The Angolan government loaned UNAVEM two helicopters and one transport plane, but this was, at best, a stopgap measure. The UN helicopters, contracted from Russia, did not arrive in Angola until the middle of June, concluding one of the more frustrating chapters of the Angolan peace process.[31]

Despite these obstacles, the UN observers were gradually deployed to sites throughout Angola, and by the end of January, twenty-eight of the fifty-three sites had been established, plus six regional headquarters. The deployment was virtually completed by the end of February. While not nearly as fast as the Angolans or UNAVEM would have liked, it was not that bad considering the logistical constraints.

How effective were the observers? On one level, they faced a "mission impossible." Their areas of responsibility were too large to be effectively monitored. As mentioned, they lacked adequate transport, especially helicopter support. Often the observers were denied access to areas within their jurisdiction, and this interfered with their patrolling and investigatory responsibilities. For the most part, they lived in desolate circumstances and often succumbed to malaria or other illnesses, as well as being exposed to land mines or random violence. One team site was overrun by unknown assailants and the observers had to be evacuated. Especially troubling were incidents in which UNITA shot at UN aircraft and helicopters. Since the observers were drawn from many different nations, language was another problem. I can remember visiting Kuito/Bié and passing by the quarters of the UN observer team. Soon I was in conversation with a diverse group representing five nationalities; only one of them could speak Portuguese, the universal language of Angola!

Yet the observers did make a difference. They carried out patrols and investigated cease-fire violations, more often than not finding the claims by the government and UNITA to be grossly exaggerated or simply not true. For tactical reasons, both sides liked to cry wolf and to blame the other for catastrophic events. Even if many minor incidents escaped the attention of the observers, they carried out a number of major investigations, however belatedly in some instances, and reported their findings to the Joint Commission. In this way, the mechanism provided a safety valve. Sometimes the observers displayed exceptional courage and diplomacy; in Huambo, for example, the UNAVEM regional commander, an Indian colonel, single-handedly stopped a potentially nasty fight and got the two forces to disengage.

The observers brought something else to the peace process. By simply being present throughout the country, they provided psychological assurance to the parties and the population at large that no one was standing alone. Although the observers were subsequently overshadowed by the arrival of the Blue Helmets, we should not overlook the importance of the observers in consolidating the cease-fire during the first phase.

Another explosive issue was disentangling the two armies where they were living cheek to jowl. There was a real concern that these flash points could ignite and blow the cease-fire apart, either by accident or by design. When the mediation team visited Uíge in January, the two forces were so close to each other—only about a hundred yards apart in some places—that it was easy to see how hostilities could break out at a moment's notice. Compounding the problem, the military commanders on both sides were hawks and looked the part; their troops also seemed tough and ready to fight.

In an effort to deal with this situation, the chiefs of staff of the FAA and FALA, Generals de Matos and Ben Ben, met in Chipapa under UN auspices on January 10. At the end of their discussion, they issued a joint declaration covering a wide range of subjects—military prisoners, hostile propaganda, triangular communications, UNAVEM access—but the disengagement of forces topped the list, especially in the priority areas of Huambo and Uíge.[32] Although the Huambo disengagement was settled fairly quickly (at least by the Angolan calendar), the disengagement in the Uíge region took much longer, in part because the government forces had moved into some of the areas vacated by UNITA in the Huambo region, which led to cries of foul play. Seemingly undeterred, the FAA later did the same thing when the Uíge redeployment was completed. Despite these problems, several months later I traveled by road from Uíge to Negage, a distance of about twenty kilometers, and saw that some progress was being made in consolidating the cease-fire between government- and UNITA-controlled territories.

SHOW THE FLAG

I made an effort to get out of Luanda as much as possible to see first-hand the enormous destruction of the war and its impact on the lives of ordinary Angolans. The visits also provided an opportunity to meet with representatives of nongovernmental organizations (such as Save the Children, World Vision, and Africare) working in the field. Living under difficult, often dangerous conditions, these young men and women helped save countless lives and provided a bedrock of support to the local populations.

Beye shared the view that it was important to travel into the countryside and to show the Angolan people that the Joint Commission was not a disembodied mechanism located somewhere in Luanda. A one-man marching band, he conducted Joint Commission meetings in various provincial capitals: the first in Huambo took place amid a tumultuous rainstorm whose thunderclaps added dramatic effect to the rancorous exchanges hurled across the table. The scene could have been taken from a novel by Joseph Conrad or V. S. Naipaul.

Beye took the Troika observers on inspection visits throughout Angola, preaching the gospel of peace as spelled out in the Lusaka Protocol. After visiting Uíge in January, the mediation team went to the fabled former headquarters of UNITA in Jamba, three and a half hours by air from Luanda. The trip was intended to demonstrate that the United Nations and observer countries were as interested in the conditions of life in UNITA-controlled areas as those in government areas, since this was a source of constant UNITA complaint. On their arrival, the visitors received a rousing welcome. A special program of speeches, plays, and traditional dances was presented. Commenting on the music, I wrote:

> A somewhat ragtag but determined military band played martial music, spurred on by the drummer who somehow managed to throw one of his batons high in the air and retrieve it, while gyrating in circles and thumping the drum exactly on beat.

I also noted the "release of two doves by the children's contingent who held placards, sometimes upside down, that contained only one word, 'Paz' or 'Peace.'" We toured the clean but rudimentarily equipped hospital and VORGAN, UNITA's radio station, whose spartan buildings housed antiquated equipment. But the station still functioned, more often than not spewing out a lot of vitriol, despite shortages of fuel supplies. Jamba was a spread-out, well-organized guerrilla encampment, carefully planned and camouflaged to protect against air attacks. But its time had passed with the end of the Cold War and the collapse of the apartheid regime in South Africa.

It is difficult to gauge what was accomplished by these forays into the countryside. We hoped they had some impact on local leaders and populations. If nothing else, they kept the sights of the mediators focused on the realities of Angola and the difficulties of translating the decisions of the Joint Commission into concrete results on the ground.

ENGAGEMENT OF THE LEADERS

During the month of January 1995, the Joint Commission wrestled with two basic problems. The first was to consolidate the cease-fire. Of equal importance was the need to arrange a meeting between Dos Santos and Savimbi. This meeting had major symbolic and political significance, since Savimbi had not come to Lusaka for the signing of the protocol. His absence and the lack of follow-up contact between the two leaders created a large void, raising doubts among Angolans and foreign observers about the future of the protocol. How could anyone believe that the peace process had real meaning unless the two leaders met and sent a joint message of peace and reconciliation to the Angolan people and the international community?

As an initial step, the Joint Commission decided that it would first meet with Dos Santos in Luanda and then with Savimbi in Bailundo. The meeting with President Dos Santos was scheduled for January 16 and with Savimbi for January 26, 1995. On the morning of the scheduled meeting with the Angolan president, the mediation team was unexpectedly informed that the meeting would not take place and that the government had asked instead for a special session of the Joint Commission. During the session, Higino explained that the president did not consider a meeting with the Joint Commission appropriate because of public statements by Savimbi and UNITA officials that cast serious doubt about their commitment to the Lusaka Protocol, as well as the alarming number of military incidents that had been initiated by UNITA following the Chipipa chiefs of staff meeting. Higino feared the peace process might be derailed unless UNAVEM took strong action to put it back on track.

In contrast to Higino's gloomy, somewhat menacing declarations, Samakuva, UNITA's chief representative on the Joint Commission, responded calmly. He expressed surprise that the government had called for a special session and pointed out that any cease-fire violations that might have been committed by one side or the other should be investigated by the UNAVEM observer teams. As for Savimbi's statements, the UNITA president had simply expressed his concerns about the process, which were quite natural considering the events at the end of last year (when the government had carried out its military offensives after the Lusaka Protocol had been initialed). Samakuva concluded that if the problems confronting the peace process were overdramatized, their resolution would be made that much more difficult. His message of restraint resonated well with the mediators, who were a bit perplexed by the government's action.

Why did the government decide to throw cold water on the peace process at this time? While both sides accused the other of cease-fire violations, the overall situation was relatively calm. The UN secretary-general reported to the Security Council on February 1 that "the UNAVEM observers have established that such violations have not been significant" and that many of the incidents involved troops foraging for food.[33] In fact, the government was principally concerned about Savimbi's publicly expressed ambivalence toward the Lusaka Protocol and had wanted to give UNITA and the mediators a jolt.

MEETINGS WITH SANTOS AND SAVIMBI

Amid these growing tensions on the political front, Beye visited Bailundo on January 18. Two days later, I saw Dos Santos and immediately afterward flew to Bailundo to see Savimbi. As usual, Dos Santos was calm and collected. He wanted the Security Council to authorize the sending of Blue Helmet infantry units and cautioned against putting too many restrictions on their deployment. He also wanted to meet with Savimbi but thought that the meeting should take place inside Angola. While the president claimed to be cautiously optimistic about the future, he was concerned about the multiplication of UNITA-initiated military incidents, which raised the question of whether UNITA was headed toward peace or war. I left the Futungo, the presidential compound, persuaded that President Dos Santos remained committed to the peace process, even if he was prepared to play a tough game.

In contrast to the quiet of the president's office, the meeting in Bailundo was long, lasting more than four hours, and action-packed. There was a definite routine to the UNITA meetings, which were as carefully scripted as a Hollywood production. After the initial greetings, each member of UNITA's inner circle presented his views on the current situation, and these views often bordered on the apocalyptic. During this first visit, General Ben Ben, Paulo Gato, Abel Chivukuvuku, Marcial Dachala, Smart Chata, Eugenio Manuvakola, Antonio Dembo, and Jorge Valentim each had the opportunity to lambaste the government's perfidies. When they were finished, Savimbi said he was pleased by the strong statements of his colleagues, which sent a powerful message to Washington. Above all, he wanted to put the Lusaka Protocol back "on the rails" and to prevent a repetition of the past. Savimbi's tone was distinctly more accommodating and positive than that of his lieutenants.

During our private meeting, Savimbi mentioned the problems created by the government's use of mercenaries, its massive arms purchases, and its recruitment efforts. Despite these difficulties, Savimbi said he was prepared to meet with Dos Santos, but he believed the two sides should first discuss the agenda so that the meeting could be constructive and achieve positive results. He was ready to send a team to Luanda at any time for this purpose. When Savimbi commented that the meeting should be held outside Angola, I demurred, saying it would have much more impact if it took place inside Angola. I also talked about the need for him to speak publicly in support of the Lusaka Protocol. Savimbi replied that the upcoming UNITA party congress would be important in consolidating support for the peace process within UNITA ranks, which had been badly fractured following the government's offensives late last year. Although the government's military actions had thrown UNITA into disarray and had put Savimbi in a difficult position, I was convinced that he remained fully in control of UNITA. He gave every appearance of an African chief who had complete dominion over his followers.

UNITA'S PARTY CONGRESS

The UNITA congress, which met during the first part of February, sent mixed signals about precisely where UNITA stood. According to press reports, Savimbi dressed down Samakuva before the assembled delegates.[34] Eugenio Manuvakola, the party's secretary general and signatory of the Lusaka Protocol, was removed from office. These were not auspicious signs. In his opening speech, Savimbi reportedly expressed reservations about the Lusaka Protocol, though he neither rejected nor endorsed the protocol outright.[35] When asked about the peacekeepers, he said:

> Are the Blue Helmets part of Angola's fabric? The answer is no. When have Angolans remained alone, united, and able to tolerate each other's differences without using tanks, aircraft, and Kalashnikovs to subjugate one another? Am I saying that Blue Helmets are unnecessary? Maybe. Maybe. Please note my exact words. Savimbi said in Bailundo: Maybe. I repeat: Maybe. They will be here for a limited period, then they will have to leave. How are we Angolans going to live after they leave? Will we once again resort to tanks, mercenaries, and Kalashnikovs?[36]

Despite these ambiguous signals, the final UNITA communiqué was artful and, on the whole, positive.[37] Among the twenty-one resolutions adopted at the congress, five had special importance. The first resolution approved all peace plans for Angola but did not specifically mention the Lusaka Protocol; the third offered qualified encouragement for the meeting between Dos Santos and Savimbi; the fourth thanked the United Nations, the observer states, and Zambia for their contribution to peace in Angola; the fifth welcomed the decision of the Security Council to send peacekeepers to Angola; and the sixteenth declared that UNITA would participate in a government of national unity only if a joint program agreed to between the parties was established. Otherwise, UNITA would prefer to be an opposition party. Interestingly, the Voice of Resistance of the Black Cockerel had this to say about the deliberations of the congress:

> Without Savimbi's intervention during the plenary session, points 3, 4, and 5 would have been rejected by the UNITA congress. The UNITA leader was able to convince the military and grass-roots militants to budge from their radical stands on the upcoming meeting between Savimbi and the President of the Republic Jose Eduardo Dos Santos, the role of the United Nations, and the sending of Blue Helmets to Angola.[38]

The government was not satisfied with the UNITA communiqué. The MPLA information secretary, João Lourenco, told the press that "UNITA must clearly and unequivocally pronounce itself in favor of or against the Lusaka accord."[39] Lourenco also pointed out that UNITA's demand for a jointly approved program for the national unity government was not mentioned in the Lusaka Protocol and that this qualification created potential complications, as it implied that UNITA could pick and choose among the various pieces of the peace agreement.

When I saw Savimbi and his colleagues later in February, I told them that the party congress had basically been positive but that a clear-cut endorsement of the Lusaka Protocol was still needed to remove any lingering doubts in the eyes of the Angolan people and the international community about UNITA's commitment to the peace process. The UNITA leaders assured me that they had no intention of changing the protocol, and Savimbi stressed that he remained fully committed to the peace process.

FEBRUARY 8 SECURITY COUNCIL RESOLUTION

The Lusaka Protocol was constructed on the assumption that a substantial peacekeeping force would be sent to Angola. Would the Security Council authorize such a large-scale mission? This was not an easy question to answer. At the beginning of February, the ceasefire, while holding, was still fragile, and the political commitment of the parties remained in doubt. The government's offensives following the initialing of the protocol had raised questions about its ultimate intentions, while UNITA's position remained unclear. Under these circumstances, the dispatch of a large peacekeeping force had political and financial risks. Beyond these specific considerations involving Angola itself, the perceived failure of the UN peacekeeping mission in Somalia raised further questions about the wisdom of engaging the United Nations in yet another African battlefield.

From the perspective of the field, the choice was clear. If the Security Council delayed the authorization of the peacekeeping mission, it would be disastrous for the peace process and could even lead to a resumption of war. Beye and Rocha-Paris were especially worried about the possibility of Security Council inaction. While I agreed with my colleagues, I also noted the difficulties of getting the Security Council to act positively in light of the unsettled situation inside Angola. I knew that many people in Washington were also concerned about the risks and costs involved in this kind of operation. In his report to the Security Council, the secretary-general supported the position of the special representative and recommended the immediate establishment of UNAVEM III for an initial period of twelve months.[40]

The Security Council straddled the fence. On the one hand, Security Council Resolution 976 (8 February 1995) authorized the establishment of the peacekeeping operation for an initial six-month period with a maximum deployment of 7,000 military personnel, in addition to the 350 military observers and 260 police observers previously approved. It also authorized the immediate deployment of planning and support elements to prepare for the arrival of the peacekeeping force. On the other hand, it placed conditions on the actual deployment of the infantry units, requiring, for example, an effective cessation of hostilities, an exchange of military data, the designation of quartering areas, and the fulfillment of a number of other military tasks.

Beye and the Troika observers were satisfied with the Security Council resolution on the assumption that once the peacekeeping train had left the station, it would be difficult to stop. Following the adoption of UNAVEM III, I wrote to Washington:

> Despite the difficulties and challenges, the room for maneuver by both sides is decreasing each day. The decision on UNAVEM III poses a further major constraint upon them. It will be difficult for either

party to back out of the process at this stage, though they will posture for every possible advantage along the way.

Neither side has attractive options. If war were to resume, the government would confront even greater societal and economic problems, already staggering. UNITA would have to go back into the bush and fight a war where it could no longer hope to achieve strategic advantage.[41]

THE JOINT COMMISSION'S TRIP TO BAILUNDO

Despite my relatively rosy assessment, the peace process nearly went off the rails completely following the decision by the Security Council. On February 13, UNITA troops shot at a UNAVEM helicopter in Quibaxe, Cuanza Norte province, forcing the helicopter to land and detaining the crew for several hours.[42] Because of the gravity of the incident, the secretary-general sent a strong letter of protest to Savimbi, and the Joint Commission held a special session to investigate the matter. UNAVEM also continued to experience difficulties in gaining access to UNITA areas. While the disengagement of forces in Huambo was completed by mid-February, the Uíge disengagement was stalled, leading the UN force commander, General Garuba, to say publicly that UNITA was not serious about carrying out the commitments it had made.[43] Garuba's remarks drew a sharp rebuke from UNITA headquarters in Bailundo.

On February 16, *Le Monde* published a bellicose interview with General João de Matos, the chief of staff of the FAA, in which he is reported to have said, "When UNITA states it wants peace, it is trying to sell to international opinion an image that does not match reality. . . . In this country, only the total military defeat of Savimbi can assure peace. . . . Those were not military men who signed the Lusaka accords but political leaders."[44] Meanwhile, de Matos deployed his armed forces and transported military equipment throughout Angola without obtaining prior authorization from UNAVEM, as was required under the protocol. General Ben Ben was also accused of making warlike statements, compelling Beye to chastise both military leaders publicly.[45]

On February 24, tempers reached a flash point. During an hour-long press interview in Luanda, a UNITA defector, Lieutenant

Colonel Zavarra, alleged that Savimbi had met with his military commanders following UNITA's party congress in Bailundo to map out a war campaign.[46] According to Zavarra, Savimbi said the Lusaka Protocol was worthless and the only path was armed struggle. Zavarra also claimed that two hundred South African military instructors had already arrived in Angola to assist UNITA and that an international force of mercenaries numbering one hundred thousand would come to Angola to take part in the new war. While UNITA did not deny that Zavarra had been a member of UNITA, it ridiculed his story.[47] That was not difficult to do, considering the inflated numbers Zavarra had cited.

More worrisome was whether the government was seriously considering the war option. When DeJarnette saw Savimbi on March 20, the UNITA leader expressed concern that the government army would strike against UNITA before the arrival of the peacekeepers. Ten days later, when I went to Bailundo, much of the discussion was devoted to reported government overflights and strafing of the Andulo airport, a traditional UNITA stronghold in the central highlands. One of UNITA's hawkish generals said the Andulo attack was "a message of war," and Savimbi stated flatly, "No air strikes will be accepted." When I saw de Matos the next day, he did not conceal his skepticism about the peace process and claimed both sides were preparing for war. Referring to the Andulo incident, I pointed out that if the overflights continued, they would inevitably lead to the explosion that he had predicted. The general said the order would be rescinded.

Still, everything was not on the dark side of the moon. UNITA took steps in March to improve UNAVEM access to its areas. Specific instructions were issued to UNITA troops to respect UN personnel, vehicles, and aircraft. The Uíge disengagement was finally completed, though the UN force commander publicly criticized the FAA for moving into some of the areas vacated by UNITA.[48] During my meeting in Bailundo in late March, the UNITA leadership went to great lengths to demonstrate their commitment to the Lusaka Protocol.

My private discussion with Savimbi was also positive. I asked Savimbi to make a clear public statement in support of the Lusaka Protocol and to invite the Joint Commission to Bailundo, including the

Angolan press corps, which had previously been barred from visiting UNITA headquarters. I said these steps would go a long way toward removing uncertainties about UNITA's commitment to the peace process and would set the stage for the long-awaited meeting between him and Dos Santos. Savimbi appeared receptive to my suggestions and said he would discuss these matters with his Political Commission the next day.

Savimbi followed through on our conversation. On April 7, the Joint Commission, accompanied by a large press contingent, traveled to Bailundo. The atmosphere was excellent. Beye declared that the date of April 7 would be inscribed in the annals of Angolan history. Savimbi spoke about the very good letter that he had just received from President Dos Santos suggesting that the two leaders meet and announced that he intended to reply in the same spirit, as one brother to another. In order to remove any lingering doubts about his support for the Lusaka Protocol, Savimbi called on both delegations to repeat after him, "We respect the Lusaka Protocol!" several times and in unison for the benefit of the press corps and television cameras. Following the public ceremony, the observers each met separately with Savimbi. When my turn came, Savimbi said, "You see that I know how to listen."

MAY 6 LUSAKA SUMMIT

The Bailundo meeting paved the way for the much sought after meeting between Dos Santos and Savimbi, which it had now been decided would be held in Lusaka where the peace agreement had been signed. Shortly afterward, UNITA sent a team, headed by Jorge Valentim, to prepare for the meeting. Added impetus came when Mobutu, Savimbi, Beye, and Essy (concurrently the foreign minister of the Ivory Coast and the president of the UN General Assembly) met in Gbadolite, Zaire, on April 14. The press communiqué issued after the meeting talked about UNITA's "irreversible support for the peace process" and the urgent need to have "a direct and fraternal" meeting between President Dos Santos and Dr. Savimbi.[49]

Despite these promising developments, the plans for the Lusaka summit nearly came unglued when we received information indicating that a UNITA team was in South Africa to prepare for a meeting between Mandela and Savimbi. Although Beye and the observers had previously urged Savimbi to meet with Mandela, the timing could not have been worse. If Savimbi met with Africa's preeminent leader and world statesman just before the proposed meeting in Lusaka, we were convinced that the government would cancel the summit out of pique. A message pointing out these difficulties was sent to Mandela, who agreed that his meeting should take place following the Lusaka summit, not before. The problem was that Savimbi was already en route to South Africa. When he was informed that the meeting had been postponed, he was furious. Beye and I were blamed for torpedoing the meeting.

With feelings running dangerously high, Beye and I agreed that we should see Savimbi personally in order to clear up any misunderstandings, though we knew we would be going into the lion's den. We flew to Bailundo on April 27. The meeting lasted five and a half hours. Except for some previous meetings with Begin, Shamir, and Sharon in Israel, I have never participated in such an explosive encounter.

Eyes flashing with anger, Savimbi heaped abuse on Beye in an hourlong, nonstop monologue, during which he recalled parts of his life story and meetings with the world's great leaders, including Presidents Reagan and Bush. He belittled Mali and Beye's role in the Angolan peace process and claimed that Beye was only interested in advancing his career while sacrificing the interests of the people of Angola. Savimbi maintained that he had not asked for the appointment with Mandela, but Thabo Mbeki, South Africa's first vice president, had insisted. If Mandela and Mbeki wanted a meeting, Savimbi said, "Do I have to ask Beye? I am not yet your slave." At several points in the monologue, the UNITA leader asserted it was a good thing I had come with Beye; otherwise, the meeting would have only lasted thirty minutes and would have been much worse.

Savimbi's lieutenants then entered the fray. The following are snippets from their extended remarks:

PAULO GATO: You can't treat Savimbi like *n'importe qui*. You can't manage the president's calendar.

JORGE VALENTIM: We haven't finished the agenda for the meeting in Lusaka. I am surprised that Beye went to Lusaka

	[to make arrangements] without contacting UNITA first. Dos Santos does not want peace, the meeting in Lusaka, or the Blue Helmets.
ALCIDES SAKALA:	Perhaps Beye gained set but not the match [said mockingly].
MARCIAL DACHALA:	You are searching for a medal; we are seeking our destiny.
SMART CHATA:	Everyone wants to help peace in the region. Why doesn't Beye want to help them? Is the special representative trying to sabotage peace [implying Beye is on somebody's payroll]?
CHIVUKUVUKU:	It is difficult to find the words. Does Beye think he is emperor or king?
ALTINO "BOCK":	We can't accept how you are treating our president. If the purpose [of the meeting in Lusaka] is to prepare a booby trap, it must be well analyzed. Otherwise, it is better not to move ahead. It would be better to die together.

Throughout these bombastic proclamations, Beye maintained his composure, though my blood was boiling. When I finally had the chance to comment, I said that I was distressed that my friend and colleague, who had worked tirelessly for peace in Angola, was being subjected to such gratuitous criticism. Later, when Paulo Gato impugned American motives, I angrily (and deliberately) threw my pencil on the coffee table and stated that as a representative of the president I refused to accept the insult.[50] Savimbi immediately intervened to calm things down, and the remainder of the meeting was conducted on a much more even keel.

Despite the Sturm und Drang, the session helped to keep the Lusaka meeting on track. Although Savimbi raised various issues and problems relating to the organization of the summit, he did not want it derailed. Subsequently, both sides confirmed that the meeting would be held in Lusaka on May 5. In the ever competing quest for scoring protocol points, the government portrayed the trip as an official visit to Zambia, during which the Angolan president would incidentally meet with the leader of UNITA. While this maneuver might appear childish, it did have its purpose. UNITA wanted the meeting in Lusaka to be seen as one between equals. Holding the meeting outside Angola strengthened this perception, as would have a prior meeting between Mandela and Savimbi. While the government agreed to hold the meeting in Zambia, it still wanted to demonstrate that it was the legal and recognized government of Angola and therefore ranked number one in protocol status.

At the last minute, a few final problems arose, and the Lusaka meeting almost did not take place, after all. Denied his trip to South Africa, Savimbi visited the Ivory Coast and Morocco, two traditional allies, before going to Lusaka. The original plan called for Savimbi to arrive in Lusaka on May 4 and Dos Santos the next day. But Savimbi did not arrive in Lusaka on schedule, and Beye was mired in Zaire without transportation and out of contact.

When Rocha-Paris and I arrived in Lusaka on the afternoon of May 4, total confusion reigned. At the airport, we saw General Kopelipa, who was trying to find out where Savimbi and Beye were. Kopelipa was visibly upset. In addition to not knowing the whereabouts of Savimbi and Beye, he showed us a letter that President Dos Santos had just received from King Hassan II of Morocco. Based on the king's recent discussions with Savimbi, the letter, which mentioned mercenaries and other security issues, seemed almost calculated to raise the hackles of the government. As the hours passed with no word from or sight of Savimbi and Beye, Kopelipa was increasingly inclined to recommend to Dos Santos that the meeting be canceled. Rocha-Paris and I counseled patience, arguing that too much was at stake to back out at the last moment. Our advice did not have much effect. On the morning of May 5, the government announced that the president's visit to Zambia was being called off.

When Beye finally got to Lusaka late at night on May 4, he did everything he could to get the meeting back on track. Savimbi, who had finally arrived in the early hours of May 5, was persuaded to stay in Lusaka an additional day. With this commitment in hand, the government was told that it would be most unfortunate if this much anticipated meeting was sabotaged at the last moment. Beye, the Zambian foreign minister, and the Troika also said they were prepared to deliver this message directly to Dos Santos in Luanda. This step proved unnecessary. During the morning of May 5, the mediation team received word that the Angolan president would come to Lusaka the next day.

After all of these ups and downs and near brushes with disaster, the meeting went surprisingly well. On a beautiful sunny day, a large crowd of journalists, UNITA officials, and Angolan and Zambian ministers gathered on the grounds of State House, the official office and residence of the president of Zambia. The ministers were there to hold bilateral talks, the presumed reason for President Dos Santos's visit, though those talks never took place. Everyone knew they were a charade. All eyes were focused instead on what was happening inside State House. After a short meeting among Chiluba, Dos Santos, and Savimbi, the Zambian president left the two Angolan leaders alone. When Chiluba returned an hour later, Dos Santos and Savimbi asked to spend more time together. The word filtering to the outside was that the talks were going well.

The private meeting lasted more than one and a half hours, following which Chiluba and the two Angolan leaders met the press. The mood was upbeat. President Dos Santos said, "No one here is frowning or crying. This is a sign that we Angolans who met in Lusaka today have been able to overcome our difficulties, to discuss our differences at length, and to reach agreement on all of the issues that were raised. . . . We are partners who have decided to work together to ensure that all of the Lusaka Protocol's clauses are implemented."[51] Savimbi responded, "This is an historic occasion . . . the President of the Republic of Angola received me very cordially. We spoke as brothers. . . . I told the President of the Republic that he is the president of my country and therefore my President."[52] With this quid pro quo between president and partner, the bargain between the two leaders was sealed.

Later in the day, Beye and the observers called on Dos Santos and Savimbi to say farewell. Both leaders confirmed that the private meeting had gone very well; in fact, it had gone much better than expected. They said in almost identical words that the person they had talked to was different from the one they had known before.

As I told the *Washington Post*, "This was just what we needed."[53] The meeting did not solve all the problems or make the peace process irreversible, but it did reinvigorate the Lusaka Protocol and raise the hopes of the Angolan people and the international community that this time the peace might endure.

6

─────────────────■·■·■─────────────────

The Arrival of the
Blue Helmets

Security Council Resolution 975 of February 8, 1995, which authorized a peacekeeping mission for Angola, was heralded as the
beginning of a new era. But the actual sending of peacekeepers to
Angola was delayed for several months thereafter. It was not until
April 20 that an advance party of the British logistical battalion, augmented by a contingent of Welsh Guards seventy strong, docked at
the port of Lobito. The first infantry battalion from Uruguay arrived
during the first week of June, almost one and a half months later.
What had happened during the intervening four months?

Part of the problem stemmed from the shakiness of the cease-fire
and the slow implementation of the Lusaka Protocol. Each side
accused the other of bad faith. During a meeting with President
Robert Mugabe in Harare, Zimbabwe, at the beginning of March
1995, the Angolan foreign minister, Venâncio de Moura, accused Savimbi of trying to plunge the country back into civil war.[1] On March 6,
the Council of Ministers declared that there had been an almost
complete lack of implementation of the Lusaka Protocol by UNITA.
The government claimed UNITA had committed 551 cease-fire violations and killed 233 soldiers and 762 civilians since the peace
treaty was signed. In the meantime, according to the government,
the United Nations was doing "empty work."[2] Dos Santos asked the
secretary-general to establish a deadline, following which a second
package of sanctions against UNITA should be considered, if UNITA
continued with the "same obstructionist attitude."[3] During a visit to

Namibia on March 10, Dos Santos underscored this negative view when he proclaimed "the peace process is in danger."[4]

UNITA adopted a more measured stance. In a communiqué issued by the office of the UNITA president on March 6, it expressed dismay at the foreign minister's statement in Harare and accused the government of preparing to launch large-scale military offensives against Bailundo, Lusamba, Negage, and Andulo. The communiqué listed a number of steps that UNITA had taken to promote the peace process, including, interestingly, the statement that "the UNITA president is so committed to the peace process that he has been forced to change the entire northern military command, specifically in Uíge." The reference was to General Abilio José Kamalata "Numa" who had been particularly obstreperous in his dealings with UNAVEM and had been instrumental in delaying the disengagement of forces in the Uíge and Negage area. The communiqué concluded by saying that the peace process was on the right track and there were no grounds for pessimism, unless the government's "virulent and malicious rhetoric" had another purpose.[5]

Although cease-fire violations remained at a relatively low level (despite the allegations on both sides), the secretary-general continued to raise the alarm. On April 7, the same day that the Joint Commission was in Bailundo, Boutros-Ghali sent a report to the Security Council stating: "More than four months after the signing of the Lusaka Protocol, there are still many causes for serious concern, namely the fragility of the cease-fire, reports of military preparations and major troop movements and indications of the continued acquisition of weapons from abroad."[6] The secretary-general exhorted both sides to take additional concrete steps to enhance the credibility of the peace process.

Another problem related to logistics and the provision of essential services and facilities for the deployment of the UN peacekeepers. Most of the responsibility in this area fell on the government. The secretary-general's report of April 7 described the lack of accommodation, office space, and warehouses and the failure to provide fuel at preferential rates, as well as not beginning the demining operation or repair of major access roads. The Status of Forces Agreement (SOFA), which spelled out the rights and obligations of UNAVEM in

Angola, had also not been signed. Most troublesome was the denial by the government of access to Catumbela airport, a major military airfield located near the port of Lobito. The United Nations needed access to Catumbela in order to fly the infantry units into Angola, but the government procrastinated. While a number of pretexts were cited, the government's refusal carried sinister overtones because the airfield was the major staging base for air operations into the central highlands and would be an important base if an offensive against UNITA were launched. At one point, the FAA even refused to allow UNAVEM officers onto the airfield, prompting the UN force commander to declare that "they often acted as though they did not give a damn about the UN mission."

The government reacted angrily to the secretary-general's report, insisting it was in full compliance with the Lusaka Protocol and claiming it had made available to UNAVEM everything that had been asked, including the use of Catumbela air base. In fact, though, the government acceded to the Catumbela issue only after the secretary-general's report had been issued. A government communiqué also indicated that the SOFA accord would be signed by April 15, thus finally disposing of this nettlesome problem.[7] The government was clearly stung by the criticism emanating from New York, even though Higino subsequently tried to downplay the problem, saying Catumbela had been "much ado about nothing."

DECISION TO DEPLOY THE PEACEKEEPERS

According to the original timetable approved by the Security Council on February 8, the deployment of the infantry units was to begin on May 9. In his report to the Security Council of March 5, the secretary-general indicated that this timetable would be met only if he were able to inform the council not later than March 25 that the deployment of the peacekeepers could take place under reasonably secure conditions. Thus, March 25 became another key benchmark in the Angolan peace process and acted as a pressure point on the parties, the Security Council, and the secretary-general himself. The president of the Security Council issued a statement on March 10 endorsing the secretary-general's conclusions and underlining the urgency of moving ahead: "Time is short if the opportunity created by the Lusaka Protocol and the Council's resolution 976 (1995) is not to be lost."[8]

Before making a decision with such portentous consequences, Boutros-Ghali dispatched his special adviser, Under Secretary General Ismat Kittani, to Angola to make an on-the-spot assessment of the peace process. Kittani visited Angola from March 17 to 22 and met with a number of government and UNITA officials, including Dos Santos and Savimbi. Both leaders told Kittani that they were fully committed to the implementation of the Lusaka Protocol and wanted an accelerated deployment of UN peacekeepers. The Troika ambassadors also stressed that the deployment of the UN force should be expedited.

The question of the Blue Helmets dominated the discussion at a Troika meeting in Lisbon, Portugal, on March 24, just before the secretary-general was to make his decision known. The Portuguese argued strongly that the deployment process had to be accelerated despite the risks, believing the peace process would otherwise be doomed. The Troika laid down a number of markers for both parties. In particular, the communiqué issued at the end of the talks stressed that free access for UN personnel to all parts of Angolan territory was a prerequisite if the UNAVEM III mandate was to be successfully carried out. There was a general consensus within the Troika that while the future looked cloudy, the "least bad" decision would be to proceed with the deployment of the UN troops.

On March 25, the secretary-general sent a letter to the president of the Security Council, in which he noted some progress in meeting the military conditions that the Security Council had indicated were required for the deployment of UN forces. Boutros-Ghali also declared new impetus was needed to help overcome the mutual distrust between the parties. He then stated:

> In light of the above, and with a view to avoiding dangerous delays in the implementation of the Lusaka Protocol which might destabilize conditions on the ground, I have decided that it would be in the best interest of the peace process to proceed with preparations for the deployment of United Nations infantry units to Angola. I fully realize that there are certain risks involved in the above decision.[9]

The members of the Security Council posed no objections to the secretary-general's decision.

THE DEPLOYMENT OF THE PEACEKEEPERS

According to the Lusaka Protocol calendar, the UN peacekeepers were to be deployed within three months of the signing of the peace agreement. But Security Council Resolution 976 placed the arrival of the first infantry units three months after the adoption of the resolution on February 8—or roughly five and a half months after the Lusaka Protocol had been signed. The original timelines had been unrealistic; this was to be a continuing pattern. Because of additional delays occasioned by the secretary-general's reassessment, the British logistical battalion only became fully operational on May 10. Other support units followed, including a signals unit (Portugal), an engineer squadron (India), and a field hospital (Romania), as well as advance parties from other units.

During the visit in May of the UN assistant secretary-general for planning and support, Lieutenant General Manfred Eisele, UNAVEM made further adjustments in the deployment schedule. The first battalion from Uruguay would arrive early June, and the next two battalions, from India and Zimbabwe respectively, were scheduled to deploy during the first and second half of July. The first priority was to get the peacekeepers into the two sensitive provinces of Uíge and Huambo. The remaining infantry units were to be phased in as road networks became operational. Movement of the infantry units by air was restricted because of the cost.

In addition to a lack of helicopters—a problem that was not resolved until mid-June—the most pressing requirements were to demine the roads and repair bridges. Although the original plan had called for the government and UNITA to do the lion's share of demining, this operation got off to a slow start. The demining challenge was enormous. Angola is one of the most mine-polluted countries in the world. Millions of mines have been planted throughout the country; estimates vary as to the total figure. New mine victims average four thousand to six thousand per year. In addition to the mining problem, the government did not have the resources to repair the priority bridges and roads. Something had to be done if the deployment of the peacekeepers into the field was not to be unduly delayed. The United Nations decided to issue a contract to a South African firm (Mechem) to demine seven thousand kilometers of roads.[10] The secretary-general also authorized adding two engineering companies to provide more support for bridge and road reconstruction.

When I went back to Washington in May 1995, I told the National Security Council and State Department that the two most urgent priorities were to fund demining programs and to send bridges to Angola. Susan Rice, the director for Africa at the National Security Council, took the bull by the horns and succeeded in sending Angola thirteen Bailey bridges (temporary bridges formed of prefabricated steel truss panels). The administration also made a total contribution to the demining effort of $8.5 million in fiscal year 1995.

Despite all of these efforts, the deployment of the infantry units proceeded slowly. When the UN secretary-general visited Angola in the middle of July, Dos Santos expressed concern over the pace of the deployment and asked that all peacekeepers be fully deployed by the end of August. Savimbi delivered a similar message. It seemed the parties could at least agree on this point. Encouraged by what he saw, Boutros-Ghali stated publicly that the Blue Helmets would be fully deployed by the end of August.

This was another deadline that would not be met. Only at the end of November—eight months after the secretary-general's decision to deploy the infantry units—could he report to the Security Council that the full deployment of the military component of UNAVEM III was *virtually* complete with more than six thousand military personnel in-country.[11] Five of the six infantry battalions (Brazil, India, Uruguay, Romania, and Zimbabwe) had been deployed to their designated areas. Boutros-Ghali pointed out that the deployment of troops to the eastern parts of the country had been hindered by mined roads and bridges and called on both parties to honor their commitments to open up the road network, particularly along the main east-west supply routes.[12]

CONSTRUCTION OF THE QUARTERING AREAS

Before the first infantry units ever arrived, the location and number of quartering areas in which UNITA was to assemble its troops had been much disputed. The Lusaka Protocol had outlined only the framework, stating that for planning purposes, the number of quartering areas was expected to be at least twelve. In general, UNITA wanted more quartering areas located in areas it had traditionally controlled. The government wanted fewer assembly points, preferably at some distance from UNITA-controlled areas. After much debate, fourteen quartering locations were finally agreed to; later, a fifteenth site was added.

As the peacekeepers began to arrive in increasing numbers in June and July, attention shifted to the actual construction of the quartering sites. The logistical challenges were enormous. Beye assigned the highest priority to this task and placed the deputy special representative, Khaled Yassir, and the deputy force commander, Brigadier Y. K. Saksena, in charge of the operation. They formed a strong team. Yassir was a seasoned UN official and administrator. Saksena knew Angola well. He had served with the United Nations during the Bicesse period and had subsequently developed the UN military deployment plan for UNAVEM III.

The quartering plan called for the construction of the sites in phases, beginning in the provinces of Huambo and Uíge. The first four quartering areas were located at Vila Nova and Londumbali (Huambo); Negage (Uíge); and Quibaxe (Cuanza Norte). Each encampment was designed to hold around five thousand persons or fewer, depending on the number of troops that UNITA had declared were in the area, and would include an adjacent site for family dependents. The camps were tent cities housing communal latrines and kitchens, including an administrative area containing warehouses, registration centers equipped with computers, medical clinics, and living areas for the civilian support staff. Two private companies, Oderbrecht and Raytheon, were contracted to construct the administrative areas and to provide electricity, water, and sanitation. UNITA personnel were expected to help construct the quartering areas themselves.

In October 1995, I accompanied Yassir and Saksena on an inspection tour of the first four sites. The quartering areas at Vila Nova and Londumbali were almost completed, although the quartering process itself had not started. From the air, these camps looked impressive: white tents neatly arranged in rows; the demarcated administrative center surrounded by a barbed-wire fence; and the checkpoints and UNAVEM command posts located on the high ground to provide maximum security. On the ground, the picture was not quite so idyllic. The land had been cleared by bulldozers and looked raw and uprooted. Providing adequate amounts of fresh water posed formidable problems. The UNITA labor force complained about the quality of food and the lack of utensils. The tents, purchased from Pakistan, were of poor quality and looked woefully inadequate to protect residents against the torrential rains that were soon to begin. Fortunately, the South Africans soon provided bigger and sturdier tents, which helped to alleviate the housing problem. Plastic sheeting was used to shore up the Pakistani tents.

Negage and Quibaxe presented another picture. In Negage, the clearing of the site was just beginning, and at Quibaxe, it had not even started. The young Indian officers had only a plan, which they painstakingly described on their maps. The sites were windswept, almost forbidding, and seemed far removed from population centers and main transportation routes. It was difficult to see how the plans would ever be executed, let alone in the short time frames demanded by headquarters. A close observer of the quartering process commented on the complexity of the task:

> The difficulties involved in the construction of the QAs have perhaps been under-estimated by the international community, and by donors in particular. Many observers were ready to blame the delays on perceived UN inefficiency. However, this analysis overlooked the complexity of an environment created by decades of war, the last three years of which were of unparalleled violence. Access remains a serious problem: roads are mined, bridges down, air-strips non-operational. Labor is a political problem: in UNITA areas, the contractor is entirely dependent on UNITA for supplying casual wage labor. Communications are difficult. There are suspected mines in many of the QA sites. Security, in a country infested with armed elements, remains a constant concern. Finally, the construction of these camps involves complex

organizational issues that require the input of numerous actors. Delays and malfunctions are inevitable.[13]

FLASH POINTS

Although the parties professed to want a rapid deployment of Blue Helmets, their actions did not always correspond with their words. Sometime in July 1995, General João de Matos gave a bellicose interview to *The Guardian* in which he attacked the United Nations and Beye and accused UNITA of consistently violating the cease-fire. Warning that the government would not allow itself to be suffocated, the FAA chief of staff indicated that a return to war was very probable and could be averted only if the UN peacekeepers were deployed by August and the UNITA troops fully quartered in September.[14]

Although a second meeting between Dos Santos and Savimbi in Franceville, Gabon, on August 10, 1995, temporarily lessened tensions, the respite did not last long. On September 7, Higino announced that the government would conduct a cleanup campaign in the sensitive diamond areas in the Lundas, ostensibly to remove illegal miners and criminal elements.[15] UNITA quickly warned that if this unilateral operation were carried out, the peace process could be derailed.[16] Under strong pressure, the government backed off. Because of their strategic and economic importance, the Lundas have always been a potential flash point in Angola; execution of the government's plan would have made the resumption of war quite likely.

Although both sides accused the other of committing gross violations of the cease-fire in the following weeks, these incidents did not have the explosive implications of the projected "police" operation in the diamond-mining areas. The violations consisted mostly of small-scale attacks, ambushes, and looting. While troubling, they did not threaten the peace process itself. Commenting on the inflamed rhetoric of that time, I wrote in a telegram to Washington: "Both parties seem to delight in describing the perfidy of the other. In fact, if one took their accounts literally, the country would be going up in smoke."

Another serious setback occurred during a shooting incident at the residence of General Ben Ben in Luanda on October 14, 1995.

Although Ben Ben was not harmed, one UNITA bodyguard was injured in the foot. Ben Ben and two other UNITA generals had come to Luanda to discuss various military issues, including the number of troops UNITA would contribute to the FAA and the concept of "global incorporation."[17] The presence of high-ranking UNITA military officers in Luanda was considered a sign of UNITA's commitment to the peace process.

When I saw Ben Ben immediately after the incident, he was agitated. The shooting reignited memories of the October 1992 massacre in Luanda, during which Ben Ben was alleged to have escaped the city disguised as a woman. I tried to persuade Ben Ben and his colleagues that they should stay in Luanda, but the military team went back to Bailundo shortly thereafter, and the peace process slowed to a snail's pace. During a visit to Bailundo on October 24, Ambassador Steinberg, who had replaced DeJarnette during the summer, and I urged Savimbi to send his military team back to Luanda and to begin the quartering process. In early November, Assistant Secretary Moose delivered the same message. Savimbi responded by pledging to quarter 1,000 to 1,500 UNITA troops at Vila Nova during the month of November. He also sent Ben Ben back to Luanda on November 13.

The October 14 shooting incident generated much speculation. Some claimed that the event was staged by UNITA in order to provide a pretext for slowing down the quartering process. The government officially maintained that a stray bullet had happened to land inside UNITA's compound. UNITA thought it was a deliberate attempt on the life of its chief of staff. Whatever the explanation, the incident revealed how easily the peace process could unravel.

THE BEGINNING OF THE QUARTERING PROCESS

The quartering of UNITA troops was not a unilateral exercise, although it was frequently described that way. During my discussions with the two parties and at the Joint Commission in October, I stated that the process required reciprocal obligations from both sides. On the one hand, the FAA had to withdraw to defensive positions and to put the Rapid Intervention Police into barracks. On the other hand, UNITA had to send "real soldiers with real weapons" to the assembly points. Trying to get the parties to carry out their respective obligations was like pulling teeth—a slow, wrenching, and painful process.

Because of the Ben Ben affair, the quartering of the troops was delayed almost a month and was not officially launched at Vila Nova until November 20, which coincided with the first anniversary of the signing of the Lusaka Protocol. The initial reports were not promising. On December 1, the secretary-general announced that only 363 UNITA troops had been quartered. And the government complained that they were "boy soldiers" carrying unserviceable weapons.[18]

Another storm cloud soon appeared on the horizon. Ever since the negotiations in Lusaka when Clinton had sent his second letter to Dos Santos, an official visit of the Angolan president to Washington had been contemplated. Although Dos Santos had visited Washington following the signing of the Bicesse accords, so had Savimbi. This time the Angolan president would be received as a head of state and given full honors. The official visit was scheduled for December 8, 1995.

Despite all of the careful planning and advance preparations, the visit ran into trouble when the FAA occupied five localities around the oil town of Soyo just before Dos Santos's visit to Washington. The government claimed that it had taken these military actions to defend the oil installation against UNITA encroachments. On December 4, UNITA's Political Commission issued a communiqué condemning the government's military operations and suspending the quartering process, which had started just two weeks earlier.[19]

Washington told the Angolan government that FAA troops should immediately withdraw from the occupied sites. Just prior to the scheduled meeting at the White House, Moose saw Dos Santos at Blair House, the official residence for visiting foreign dignitaries, and made it clear that the Soyo operation had jeopardized the success of the president's visit. Dos Santos understood the seriousness of the situation. During his meeting with President Clinton, he outlined a series of steps that the government would take to bolster the peace process. They included withdrawing FAA troops from occupied positions around Soyo, putting the Rapid Intervention Police into barracks, moving FAA troops away from the quartering areas, and canceling the contract with Executive Outcomes, the South African company that had supplied the bulk of mercenaries to the Angolan government. Dos Santos's commitments, later made public, helped to clear the air, and the rest of the meeting went very well.

Why did the FAA seize the positions around Soyo on the eve of President Dos Santos's visit to Washington? The official reason, citing self-defense, was not totally convincing, nor was the speculation that the military command had carried out the mission without authorization from its political leadership. General de Matos might be outspoken but he was not inclined to conduct rogue operations. The one thing that is clear is that the Soyo incident was badly conceived and timed and provided UNITA with the perfect pretext for suspending its participation in the quartering process.

At the same time, the Dos Santos visit put the U.S.-Angolan relationship on a more solid footing. The Angolan government largely carried out the commitments that Dos Santos had made to Clinton. The contract with Executive Outcomes was terminated and its personnel returned to South Africa in January 1996, though UNITA claimed many mercenaries remained in Angola and others subsequently returned under different guises. The FAA withdrew from the positions it had occupied around Soyo, and a platoon of UN troops was deployed to the area as a confidence-building measure. Although the pace was sometimes uneven, the Rapid Intervention Police were put into barracks, and the FAA gradually (and with considerable prodding from the mediators) withdrew to defensive positions.

THE RESTARTING OF THE QUARTERING PROCESS

With the peace process basically stalled at the beginning of 1996, the mediators and the international community put renewed pressure on UNITA to quarter its troops. A flurry of diplomatic activity ensued, with messages arriving from the president of the Security Council, the UN secretary-general, and the president of Portugal. Beye and the Troika met with Dos Santos and Savimbi.

On January 18, the U.S. permanent representative to the United Nations, Madeleine Albright, arrived in Luanda. Not one for mincing words, she publicly warned that the patience of the international community was running out and that real progress in implementing the Lusaka Protocol was expected before the scheduled Security Council meeting on February 8, the first anniversary of the establishment of UNAVEM III. Otherwise, she said, the peacekeeping mandate might be put in jeopardy.[20] Albright conveyed this message directly to Savimbi the next day in Bailundo. During their private meeting, she proposed that UNITA quarter 16,500 troops by February 8, based on the calculation that each of the four opened quartering areas could process 200 soldiers a day. Savimbi agreed. After the meeting, the UNITA leader told the press, "I gave her my word on behalf of the party and the armed forces that by 8 February we will confine 16,500 troops. This word comes from an elder [*mais velho*] and war veteran. I shall keep my word."[21]

On leaving Angola, Albright said Savimbi had been told that "actions speak louder than words."[22] But did Savimbi keep his word? Not exactly. UNITA confined only about eight thousand soldiers by February 8. In explaining the shortfall, Savimbi said that fourteen thousand troops had arrived at their designated prequartering sites, but not all of them had been able to register at the quartering areas. The UNITA leader claimed logistical problems hampered the operation, including lack of transportation by the UN, but he promised to meet his public commitment to Albright within several days.[23] While expressing deep concern about the slow pace of the quartering process, the Security Council decided to extend the mandate of UNAVEM III for three months.[24]

Following this burst of activity, the pace slowed again. UNAVEM reported that only about 16,500 troops had been quartered by the end of February, or approximately the number that Savimbi had promised would be quartered three weeks earlier.[25] Both sides raised complaints about the process. The government claimed that many of the soldiers were underage or were not real soldiers. UNAVEM reported that it had received reports that UNITA was commandeering youths in the villages to send to the camps.[26] General de Matos claimed only one-third of the weapons being turned in by UNITA were usable.[27] There was some truth to his observation. When I visited the Negage quartering area a couple of months later, many of the weapons on display looked as if they had last been fired in the Boer War!

On the other side, UNITA constantly harped on the inhuman conditions in the camps resulting from poor tenting, food, and medical conditions, sometimes going so far as to call them concentration camps. Although the camp conditions were spartan, the UNITA complaints were exaggerated. A number of the soldiers and family members came to the quartering areas malnourished or suffering from a variety of diseases. For example, the United Nations reported that over twenty-five thousand pathologies were diagnosed in the first four quartering areas.[28] Once in the camps, the troops could at least expect to receive a medical checkup and a steady diet. The real problem was that the camps were constructed to hold the troops for only three to five months, during which it was anticipated that all UNITA's military would have been quartered and subsequently either incorporated into the FAA or demobilized. As the quartering process dragged on much longer than anticipated, the desertion figures began to mushroom.

The quartering process continued to languish through March and April. When progress became almost imperceptible, the government reacted. On April 23, Higino said the Joint Commission should not hold any more meetings until UNITA provided a plausible explanation for the delays, adding with his customary flourish, "We cannot sit laughing at the negotiating table every day and never see the tune change. We want to put an end to this type of behavior."[29] In its rebuttal, UNITA indicated that the slowdown was related to the lack of progress in issuing a presidential statement on amnesty. Valentim explained that UNITA needed the amnesty statement so that its military officers could join the national army on an equal footing with their brothers.[30] The government responded that this was only an excuse.[31] Although Beye and the observers did not accept the linkage between the quartering and amnesty issues, they urged the government to act promptly on the amnesty law in order to remove any pretext for further delays. The law went into effect on May 8.

During this hiatus, Ambassador Steinberg and I saw Savimbi in Andulo on April 25, and Beye met with Savimbi afterward. During the opening session of our meeting, the UNITA team raised a familiar litany of complaints about the miserable conditions in the quartering areas, security concerns, and the amnesty question. Steinberg and I explained that the slow pace of quartering UNITA's troops was raising real concerns in Washington about the future of the peace process in Angola. Looking ahead to the May 8 Security Council meeting, we stated that a jolt was needed to restore credibility and confidence.

At this point, the discussion got down to brass tacks. After some give and take with General Bock, who had overall responsibility for the quartering process on UNITA's side, we agreed that I could tell the press that UNITA would confine *at least* 30,000 troops by May 8, up from the 23,000 troops that were quartered at that time. Steinberg and I stressed that we needed "steady, consistent, and credible quartering" with the clear objective of completing the process by June, as had been agreed by Dos Santos and Savimbi during their third meeting in Libreville, Gabon, on March 1. The quality of troops quartered and weapons delivered also had to improve.

Savimbi kept his commitment. UNITA registered more than 30,000 troops in ten quartering areas by the May 8 deadline.[32] In the middle of May, Savimbi made a further promise to Beye that 50,000 troops would be quartered by June 15 and that the process would be completed by the end of June.[33] Although the June 15 deadline was met, the second half of Savimbi's commitment was not. At the end of June, 52,000 UNITA troops had been quartered, about 10,000 short of its declared total of 62,500.[34]

At this point, the numbers game became confused. Although more than 63,000 UNITA troops were registered in the camps at the end of September, UNITA indicated that 1,700 troops and 5,500 policemen still remained outside the quartering areas.[35] UNITA claimed that the UNITA police force, which had never been mentioned during the negotiations in Lusaka, was needed to provide law and order in the areas that had been vacated by UNITA's regular troops. In fact, there was little doubt that the policemen were regular troops, outfitted in blue police uniforms.

Finally, on December 11, the quartering process drew to a sputtering close when UNITA declared that all of its troops had been confined and their weapons turned over to UN peacekeepers. Even this declaration contained two caveats, however, one of which was important, the other not. The less consequential issue concerned 463 policemen who still had to be quartered. This task, according to UNITA, would be completed in the next several days. Of greater significance, the declaration stated that the presidential guard, whose numbers and weapons were not declared, would be dealt with when the special status of the UNITA president was discussed.[36]

THE ARRIVAL OF THE UNITA GENERALS

Although the major focus during 1996 was the construction of the quartering areas and the quartering of UNITA troops, the peace process also addressed other important military issues. The most prominent was the incorporation of UNITA generals into the FAA command structure. Two contentious points were involved. The first concerned how many UNITA generals would be incorporated into the army. UNITA asked for forty-nine positions, while the government countered with three. After several months of offers and counter-offers, it was finally agreed that UNITA would receive nine positions, including the deputy chief of staff.[37]

The second point concerned the timing of the UNITA generals' incorporation into the FAA. According to the Lusaka Protocol, this was to occur once the quartering process had been completed. Both parties, however, subsequently agreed that the incorporation of the UNITA generals should be accelerated in order to boost confidence and to spur the military integration process. Under this revised agreement, the generals were scheduled to arrive in Luanda in July. But like almost every other deadline, this one was not met.

On September 9, 1996, the White House announced that I would be arriving in Angola that day to underscore American concern about the continuing delays in the peace process. Whether by accident or design, the first group of UNITA generals arrived in Luanda that evening. Although it was not the full complement to which the parties had agreed, still the arrival of the generals was considered an encouraging development. Adding to the drama at the airport, Ben Ben arrived with his family and told the press that he had come to stay in Luanda permanently. The media had a field day photographing the general's children and their mother.

When the American team went to Bailundo two days later, I told Savimbi that the arrival of the UNITA generals in Luanda had been well received but urged that he send the remaining generals to Luanda quickly. The final group arrived one month later on October 11. Now, the government stalled. In an attempt to put pressure on UNITA, the government refused to incorporate the UNITA generals into the FAA until UNITA had declared that all of its troops had been quartered. The mediation team insisted that while the government's position was strictly speaking in conformity with the Lusaka Protocol, the original timetable had been supplanted by the subsequent agreement. This dispute was resolved only when UNITA issued the requested statement on December 11. The generals were incorporated into the FAA the same day and took the oath of office on December 20.

OBSERVATIONS ON THE MILITARY PROCESS

The implementation of the military accords was a herky-jerky affair. During a visit to Angola in October 1995, I reported to Washington that while it was difficult to predict what the future might hold, "my only certain prediction is that the peace process will go at a slower rate than what we and the international community want. The two timetables [Angolan and international] are not synchronized."

The problem stemmed in part from the unrealistic deadlines set by the international community and the parties themselves. Because of the substantial expenditures involved, the Security Council did not want to enter into an open-ended commitment in which the peacekeeping operation would become a permanent feature of the landscape, as had happened in Cyprus, southern Lebanon, and the Golan Heights. Fortunately, in the case of Angola, the Security Council extended the UNAVEM III mandate to February 1997, which provided a little bit of cushion to absorb the inevitable shocks and delays that were associated with implementing the accords.[38] Even so, the international calendar constantly collided with the slow pace of implementation on the ground.

Further complicating the situation was the difficulty of deploying a large peacekeeping force and constructing fifteen quartering areas. Both operations faced formidable logistical challenges, especially in opening up land routes to remote areas in the country's interior. While the UNAVEM team did a good job of dealing with these problems, the UN plans almost inevitably ran behind schedule.

The government also contributed to the delays. The problems of gaining access to the Catumbela air base and obtaining clearances for the Mechem demining teams impeded the deployment of the peacekeepers. The Soyo incident, occurring on the eve of President Dos Santos's visit to Washington, set back the quartering process. Because of the widespread conviction in government circles that UNITA only responded to pressure, the withdrawal of the FAA to defensive positions was protracted, and this provided UNITA with yet another reason to slow down the quartering of its troops.

UNITA, however, bore most of the responsibility for the delays. The simple truth was that UNITA was never enamored with the Lusaka Protocol, especially the provision calling for the disarming of its troops. The problem was fundamental, as UNITA's military arm had formed the backbone and raison d'être of the movement since 1966. Savimbi said on a number of occasions that the problem was not the confinement of his troops but the surrender of their weapons. In his darker moments, Savimbi would ask, What leader had ever given up his army and survived?

On the other hand, did UNITA really disarm? Even on the surface and without looking too far below, the evidence indicated that UNITA did not. UNITA never declared the size of the presidential guard, for example. The UNAVEM military command did not believe that UNITA had turned in all of its heavy weapons or dismantled its command and control system. UNITA openly proclaimed that it had so-called mining police in the diamond areas of the Lundas; few doubted that these were actually military forces under another name. Other reports indicated that UNITA had positioned some of its crack military units across the border in the former Zaire.

Given the long years of conflict and levels of distrust, this development did not come as a surprise. Many observers had believed that UNITA would maintain a residual military force as a form of insurance against unilateral actions by the government or the collapse of the peace process. The real question focused on intentions and capabilities. Was UNITA's purpose to retain a defensive capability only until the overall political and military situation became clearer? Or did UNITA intend to keep an offensive military capability in order to strike at the government again?

No one knew the answer to these questions. Given the paucity and conflicting nature of information available to the United Nations and the observers, we could only speculate. So much depended on the calculations and decisions of one man: Jonas Savimbi. The only proposition that seemed credible was that as the peace process moved forward in fits and starts and as the government's military power grew stronger, UNITA's room for maneuvering would steadily diminish.

7

The Political
Denouement

The Lusaka Protocol did not address several important issues. Of these, many observers believed that Savimbi's role in the transitional government was paramount because of his larger-than-life presence on the Angolan stage. The Lusaka Protocol deliberately omitted any mention of this role. While the protocol contained an article that said the president of UNITA would be guaranteed "a special status," the negotiators felt Savimbi's future role could only be resolved directly and privately between the two leaders. The issue was too sensitive and important to settle around the negotiating table in Lusaka. There was no dispute between the parties on this point.

Beginning with the Zambian delegation's meeting with Savimbi in July 1994, various possibilities about the role that Savimbi might play had been discussed. At that time, participants floated the idea of a single vice presidency position. Following the May 1995 meeting between Dos Santos and Savimbi in Lusaka, the discussion focused on two vice presidency positions patterned on the South African model. According to this proposal, UNITA would be offered the second vice presidency, since the MPLA did not want Savimbi to be in the direct line of succession should Dos Santos become incapacitated. During their second meeting in Franceville, Gabon, on August 10, 1995, President Dos Santos reported that he and Savimbi had agreed there would be one vice presidency for the MPLA and another for UNITA.

When the two leaders met again in Libreville, Gabon, on March 1, 1996, they seemed to have clinched the deal. After the meeting,

Savimbi told the press that he had received a letter from the president offering the vice president position and that he intended to respond personally or through a trusted intermediary.[1] Because of the generally positive manner in which he had described the offer, it was widely assumed that Savimbi had accepted the post. Dos Santos certainly thought so. When he was queried by the press on the subject, the president stated,

> All I can tell you is that Dr. Savimbi expressed a profound commitment to strengthening the peace and national reconciliation. Obviously, one of the ways he can help is to become part of the government, so the peace process can inspire confidence and the Angolan people can believe in the work we are doing for peace and national reconciliation. It is for this reason that I cannot believe he will reject the offer.[2]

Despite these hopeful messages, rumblings could be heard in the background reflecting a great deal of ambivalence within UNITA about the vice presidency question. As early as July 1995, the UNITA representative in the Ivory Coast, John Kakumba Marques, indicated that Savimbi would not accept a ceremonial post.[3] In the same month, Paulo Gato said in an interview, "I cannot imagine President Savimbi as deputy vice president [second vice president]. But that is only my personal opinion."[4] Following the Libreville meeting, Abel Chivukuvuku, a leading UNITA official, said in a press interview that UNITA needed to see what responsibilities would be assigned to the position before the party could decide who would be most suitable to be vice president.[5] This hardly constituted categorical support for the concept.

During a speech marking UNITA's thirtieth anniversary, Savimbi delivered a message that contrasted sharply with the optimistic spirit of the Libreville meeting just two weeks earlier and that perhaps reflected his own feelings more accurately. At one point, he asked, "Do you really need Savimbi as vice president?" to which the crowd responded (predictably) with a thunderous "No!" Continuing in the same vein, he declared, "Perhaps I will be more useful telling the truths I tell rather than going around gagged. I would also not like to die from a heart attack just because I was not received by the president's office. I can be far more useful outside the cabinet than inside it."[6] Although Savimbi cloaked his ultimate intentions in a veil of ambiguity, the message created confusion and consternation in Luanda and international circles, especially as his remarks came so soon after the perceived breakthrough at Libreville.

In the following weeks, the two parties held desultory discussions in Luanda on constitutional revisions, including the issue of the two vice presidencies. UNITA took the position that the two vice presidents should have executive powers and the prime ministership should be abolished, though its negotiators refused to give a definitive commitment that Savimbi would accept the second vice presidency. For its part, the government made it very clear that it was only offering the vice presidency to Savimbi and a substitute would not be acceptable.

From August 20 to 27, 1996, an extraordinary session of the UNITA congress was held in Bailundo to discuss the peace process in general and Savimbi's role in particular. The tone was set on the second day when Paulo Gato addressed the assembly:

> Our party cannot dispense with its leader, who is greatly needed and even irreplaceable at this stage of the struggle, which is now eminently political. The international community and the Luanda regime already have deprived us of our armed forces in accordance with UN Security Council Resolution 864/93, paragraph 8. They left us without armed forces. Now, they want to destroy our party by giving our leader a vice presidency that will keep him away from us. Are the UNITA militants in agreement with this? [Crowd replies, "No!"] Savimbi is our leader! He is our leader! He guides us![7]

If that was not enough of a signal, the congress's final communiqué categorically rejected the second vice presidency, putting an end to the proposal once and for all.[8] Although Savimbi tried to downplay the significance of the communiqué, claiming the issue was "incidental"[9] (which, of course, it was not), the government and ruling party were incensed. The MPLA Political Bureau asked the Joint Commission to invalidate the provision of the Lusaka Protocol that guaranteed Savimbi's special status; this would have put an end to further discussion of the subject.[10] Beye wisely refused to consider the request.

When I arrived in Luanda on September 9 not long after the UNITA congress, Steinberg and I met with President Dos Santos and discussed Savimbi's role. Dos Santos said he was deeply disappointed by the decision of the UNITA congress; he believed he had received a firm commitment from Savimbi to accept the vice presidential post. He was also disturbed by the fact that Savimbi had conveyed his message publicly rather than through private channels as he had promised. The public rejection was insulting and undermined the president's own position within his constituency. While sympathetic to Dos Santos's concerns, Steinberg and I indicated we still thought it was important for Savimbi to be associated with the government and to have direct access to the presidency. We suggested that Savimbi might be offered the position of "special adviser to the president," with specific responsibilities for national reconstruction. Such a position would not require constitutional revision or put Savimbi directly in the governmental hierarchy. Dos Santos's response was indirect: following the decision of the UNITA congress, he said, it was no longer up to him to make the offers.

Steinberg and I then saw Savimbi in Bailundo. We explained that his actions had been a slap in the face to the president and that he needed to take the initiative. We suggested various roles that he might play, including the post of "special adviser to the president." While claiming that the government had never provided a description of the responsibilities he would have as second vice president, Savimbi said he understood that UNITA had to take the initiative and promised to send a UNITA team to Luanda to continue the discussions.

Like so much of Angola's history, the rest of this story took a convoluted and protracted course. The dossier was put in the hands of the Joint Commission. Proposals and counterproposals were made. On September 20, UNITA proposed that as president of the largest opposition party, Savimbi should be given the status of "leader of the opposition," based on the British parliamentary model. Without prejudice to the existing line of succession, UNITA also wanted Savimbi to be number two in the protocol ranking, following the president of the republic.[11] Still piqued, the government took its time responding to this proposition. Finally, in the middle of November, it offered a counterproposal stripped of any substantive content, outlining instead a laundry list of items that would be offered to Savimbi, including a residence, driver, cook, domestics (two), first-class air tickets (two per year), and monthly salary equal to that of the prime minister.[12] The response was calculated to match UNITA's earlier rejection of the second vice presidency.

As the mediation team tried to blend the different proposals into one, another fly in the ointment appeared. In early January 1997, Savimbi went to South Africa where he held lengthy meetings with leading officials, including Nelson Mandela and Thabo Mbeki. The meetings were described as party-to-party talks between the ANC and UNITA, but they soon took on a different character. Press reports indicated that South Africa had agreed to act as a go-between to help resolve the prickly question of Savimbi's special status.[13] Savimbi welcomed South Africa's intervention, which would have bypassed the authority of the mediators and the Joint Commission.

The government reacted negatively to this news. In a speech before the diplomatic corps in Luanda on January 10, Dos Santos said, "I want to make a strong appeal to South Africa not to open new dialogue channels in the ongoing process, but merely assist the special representative of the UN secretary general."[14] Although the South Africans quickly made it clear that they had no intention of establishing a separate negotiating channel, the episode created bad feelings between the two governments. When Thabo Mbeki visited Luanda in late January, he attempted to repair the damage. He assured his interlocutors that South Africa had no intention of playing a mediating role in Angola but only wished to share with the Angolans its experiences in forming a unity government and building a spirit of national reconciliation across party lines.[15]

Savimbi's visit to South Africa also altered his view of the role that he should play in the government. He now proposed that he be given the status of "principal adviser to the president," with special responsibilities for rural development and national reconciliation, as well as supervisory powers over several ministries.[16] The government balked. The discussions went back to square one.

OTHER ITEMS ON THE POLITICAL AGENDA

Savimbi's special status was not the only subject on the political agenda during this period. Following UNITA's declaration of

December 11, 1996, on the disarming of its troops, the focus shifted to the next calendar of events. According to the Lusaka Protocol, the next step consisted of the return of UNITA's deputies to the National Assembly and the installation of the Government of National Unity and Reconciliation (GURN). The Security Council called for the formation of the new government by the end of December 1996.[17] Although the council stated that Savimbi's status should be resolved quickly, it explicitly delinked this issue from other political steps, such as the establishment of the GURN, in order to avoid another gridlock.

The Security Council's timetable was not met, nor was the revised timetable adopted by the Joint Commission in the middle of December 1996, which called for the return of the deputies by January 10 and the inauguration of the GURN by January 25, 1997. Despite the demand of the Security Council, UNITA announced that the special status for Savimbi had to be resolved before the other political steps could be implemented.[18] As the January deadlines faded, the Joint Commission agreed to a new calendar, calling for the arrival of the UNITA deputies and officials by February 12 and setting a subsequent date for the inauguration of the GURN.[19]

This new timetable also ran into trouble. When the UNITA Political Commission met in Bailundo from February 3 to 5, it expressed general satisfaction with the implementation of the Lusaka Protocol and indicated its readiness to send the UNITA deputies and officials to Luanda, but it also raised a new demand. The Political Commission stated it was imperative to hold prior discussions with the government on a common program, priorities, and the intended duration of the transitional government until a new round of elections were held.[20] Although this demand had been voiced as far back as the meeting of the party's congress in February 1995, its re-emergence at this late date aroused suspicions that UNITA was deliberately stalling.

The MPLA spokesman, João Lourenco, promptly rejected the UNITA proposal and insisted it was contrary to the provisions of the Lusaka Protocol. When asked if the UNITA officials joining the government would have to accept the government's program, Lourenco, who is known for his hard-line views, categorically stated that they would.[21]

On February 12, UNITA sent twelve deputies and four ministerial candidates to Luanda, even though no progress had been made on agreeing to a common program. Why did UNITA take this first halting step? The reason can be traced back to New York. In a statement issued by the president of the Security Council on January 30, the council took note of the new timetable adopted by the Joint Commission and stated that if this deadline was not met, the Security Council would be compelled to consider imposing sanctions against the responsible party.[22] Even though UNITA spokesmen liked to claim that the international community was biased and that UNITA was impervious to criticism or threats of sanctions, their actions seldom corresponded with this rhetoric. By sending the first group to Luanda, UNITA hoped to deflect action by the Security Council while continuing to maintain that the discussion of a common program was an important test of the government's willingness to promote real national unity and reconciliation. While one could argue over UNITA intentions, the basic premise had a certain validity.

During the rest of February, the situation remained in flux. When the new government had still not been formed at the end of February, the Security Council requested the secretary-general to provide a progress report by March 20.[23] Responding to this new deadline, UNITA sent a second group of deputies and officials to Luanda. By March 19, forty-three UNITA deputies (out of seventy) and seven officials (out of eleven) were in the capital, just enough to stem further action by the Security Council.

In his March 20 report, the new secretary-general, Kofi Annan, blamed UNITA for the repeated postponements in establishing the unity government. Sounding almost resigned, he said, "I realize the patience of the international community is wearing thin. It is in this spirit that I have decided to visit Angola from 22 to 25 March 1997 with the intention of making a first-hand assessment of the situation and impressing upon the parties the need to establish the Government of Unity and National Reconciliation without any further delay."[24]

THE VISIT OF THE SECRETARY-GENERAL

The secretary-general had originally hoped to be present for the inauguration of the new government, but as he said on his arrival, "alas there has been another slight delay—and this is one of many."[25] By this time, so many deadlines had been missed that it was difficult to keep track of events! The key stumbling block continued to be the return of the full component of UNITA deputies and officials to Luanda.

In an effort to break the impasse, Kofi Annan traveled to Bailundo on March 24. At the conclusion of the meeting, Savimbi publicly stated that the remaining UNITA deputies and officials would go to Luanda the next day, which would enable the president to establish a date for the swearing-in of the new government. Annan was delighted with the news. He was scheduled to speak before the National Assembly the next day and wanted UNITA's parliamentary delegation to be present.

But once again, things did not exactly work out according to plan. By the next morning, about twenty UNITA deputies had still not arrived in Luanda. While their absence could be excused on logistical grounds, the fact that the four key UNITA officials who were to take up ministerial positions in the government had also not shown up was more disturbing, since they had to be present in Luanda if a date for swearing in the new government was to be announced.

At this point, Savimbi's good word and credibility were at stake. He had broken solemn public commitments given to the new secretary-general the previous day. As I told Samakuva and Chivukuvuku, this was especially serious since Savimbi had given his word not only to a *new* secretary-general, but to a fellow African as well. It could only be construed as a deliberate snub.

Although the secretary-general failed to get all of UNITA's representatives to Luanda or to establish a firm date for the installation of the new government, his visit helped to bring the different pieces of the peace process together. On the eve of his arrival, the Joint Commission approved the text on the special status of Savimbi with the understanding that it would be approved by the National Assembly before the UNITA deputies took their seats in the assembly. The final compromise essentially blended the proposals that UNITA and the government had submitted to the mediation team in late 1996. Under the new formulation, instead of "leader of the opposition," Savimbi would enjoy the title of "president of the major opposition party" in recognition of the independence of the other opposition parties in the parliament. In addition, the document described briefly and succinctly Savimbi's rights and obligations. The issue of precedence was fudged by stating that Savimbi would have "a privileged position and prominence in all public acts and state protocol ceremonies." The insulting references in the original government proposal were deleted and replaced by more dignified language. Of special importance was the document's statement that its provisions could not be amended or suspended without Savimbi's approval.

After two years of entangled negotiations, the issue of Savimbi's status, which many considered to be the key to finding peace in Angola, closed on an almost anticlimactic note. While the final resolution kept Savimbi outside the formal government structure and hierarchy, it did provide a platform on which he could play an important and constructive role in Angola's political life, if he chose to do so. The question was whether he would.

In addition, on the eve of Annan's visit, the government agreed to discuss with UNITA a common program for the national unity government. The mediation team had put strong pressure on the government to hold these talks on the grounds that this relatively minor issue should not block the formation of the unity government. On a substantive level, the two sides were not far apart. UNITA had publicized its proposals on February 11. On March 3, the government had presented a draft program to UNITA, which it said would be submitted to the Council of Ministers, Angola's equivalent of the American cabinet, once the GURN was established. The government added that the draft document had taken into account the views expressed by UNITA in its February 11 proposals.[26]

Once the parties agreed to talk about the program, the discussions concluded in less than a week. In fact, the dispute was more symbolic than real. UNITA wanted to demonstrate that it was entering the new government as a partner and that its views needed to be heard. The government wanted to show that it was in charge and that UNITA was a junior partner. Despite these differing agendas, the two parties agreed to a joint program because neither wanted to be accused of blocking the installation of the GURN at the last minute.

THE FORMATION OF THE GURN

In the late evening of March 28, the last members of UNITA's team arrived in Luanda. Two designated UNITA ministers, Marcos Samondo and Jorge Valentim, were on board the UNAVEM aircraft. When the two officials stepped off the plane waving UNITA's flag, there was a palpable sigh of relief among the UN and Troika officials who could finally see this part of the peace process coming to a close. The maneuvers and delays, stretching over more than three months, had been an exhausting experience for everyone involved.

Following the arrival of the last UNITA officials, the government issued a declaration on March 31. The statement began somewhat acerbically by noting that UNITA had not fully complied with various provisions of the Lusaka Protocol, specifically by failing to withdraw from illegally occupied areas, turn over all of its military and communications equipment, and change the status of its shortwave radio station, VORGAN. Despite these drawbacks, the declaration stated that the government of the Republic of Angola would like to announce that the UNITA deputies would be sworn into office on April 9 and the new government installed on April 11.[27] The Joint Commission confirmed these arrangements the same day.

Just when everything seemed to be in place for the swearing-in ceremony, another problem arose. During its meeting on April 2, the MPLA Political Commission put a number of outstanding military and political problems on the record.[28] The tone of the commission's declaration produced a sour, accusatory note on the eve of establishing the unity government, which was ostensibly dedicated to promoting national reconciliation. Of more substantive concern was the statement from the Political Commission that Savimbi's special status should be approved only after UNITA's deputies had taken their seats in the National Assembly. Since this proposal conflicted with the prior agreement that Savimbi's status would be approved *before* the UNITA deputies were seated, it had more sinister overtones.

The new wrinkle prompted a strong reaction from UNITA. UNITA's secretary general, Paulo Gato, said the proposition was unacceptable and reflected the MPLA's "hegemonic" tendencies. With his typical propensity to overdramatize, Gato added, "We regard this as a great conspiracy against democracy in our country."[29] In fact, the suggestion probably reflected the relatively benign desire of the MPLA leadership to associate directly the UNITA deputies with the approval of Savimbi's special status.

In the end, the mediators encouraged the government to adhere to the procedure to which the Joint Commission had agreed in order to avoid another protracted round of negotiations, which would again upset the timetable for the swearing-in ceremony. The government complied, instructing its deputies to approve Savimbi's special status on April 8. It was a bittersweet moment for many MPLA deputies. According to one press report, Lucio Lara, an MPLA veteran, "described the law as an insult and broke into tears while delivering his speech."[30] The measure passed with only six abstentions. Sixty-seven UNITA deputies were sworn into office the next day.

On April 11, twenty-eight ministers and fifty-five vice ministers, including four ministers and seven vice ministers from UNITA, took the oath of office in the National Assembly building. The solemn ceremony was attended by a number of African heads of state, including Nelson Mandela, and the president of Portugal. President Dos Santos spoke movingly about the occasion:

> Today's inauguration of the GURN proves that it is still possible to successively overcome the countless hurdles that have so far prevented genuine reconciliation within the Angolan family. It was necessary after more than two decades to attain that goal. Now that we have attained it, we realize that reconciliation is nothing but the starting point for a new era. Left behind are the thousands upon thousands of dead and crippled, a needy people whose flesh and soul have been wounded, a devastated country, a semi-paralyzed economy, and various generations of despondent citizens virtually with no prospects in life.[31]

The Angolan president said the hardships that the Angolan people had endured demonstrated forever the futility of a war between brothers.

Despite the solemnity and hope symbolized by the occasion, one person's absence cast a shadow over the ceremony. Savimbi chose not to come. Instead, UNITA's vice president, Antonio Dembo, delivered a speech on behalf of the president of UNITA. Dembo's presence, though important, could not carry the same meaning or weight as Savimbi's would have.

Why did Savimbi choose not to participate in such a momentous occasion? Although UNITA cited security considerations, these were not the major reason. Even Savimbi downplayed the issue of security when he was asked why he had not attended the swearing-in ceremony:

> I was unable to go to Luanda, but I will go there soon. I must mention one fact: Many people talk of security; political leaders do not enjoy maximum security. I left Luanda in 1992 under the conditions that everyone knows. So, I cannot sneak back into Luanda. I must be welcomed there as my party's leader. Since the members of my party could not be there to welcome me at the airport, I could not go back. When everything is ready, I will go back as I did in 1991.[32]

In view of the historic importance of the event, Savimbi's explanation was not wholly convincing. A more compelling reason had to exist. According to the UNITA representative in Washington, Jardo Mukalia, UNITA wanted to avoid the impression that its leader had surrendered to President Dos Santos.[33] While this argument has a certain logic, it ultimately does not ring true. If Savimbi had come to Luanda, he would have received a hero's welcome, just as he would have if he had been present at the signing of the Lusaka Protocol in November 1994. It would not have been interpreted as a sign of weakness or surrender—quite the opposite. The real reason lay in UNITA's (and Savimbi's) continued ambivalence toward the Lusaka peace process and a desire to maintain a certain distance from it. This fit into the party's policy of keeping all options open, of moving slowly every step of the way, and of avoiding firm commitments. The strategy was deliberate and designed to keep the government—and the mediation team—off balance and guessing. By following this course, however, Savimbi risked distancing himself too far from the day-to-day life not only of the government but also of UNITA's representatives in the GURN and National Assembly.

Despite Savimbi's absence, the inauguration of the unity government marked an important milestone in the implementation of the Lusaka peace accords. UNITA members now occupied important positions in the army, police, government, and parliament and had the opportunity to participate in the political life of the country. Although the future remained uncertain, these were steps in the right direction. Much would now depend on how the MPLA members of the new government helped to foster greater openness and transparency throughout the bureaucracy and the political system, and how they welcomed their UNITA colleagues in the governance of the country.

8

■+■+■

The Unfinished
Agenda

The Angolan peace process began to change with the installation of the unity government. On July 1, 1997, the Security Council downgraded the UN peacekeeping operation to an observer mission, triggering a steady downsizing of the infantry units.[1]

Just prior to this Security Council decision, the secretary-general reported on the status of the peace process in Angola.[2] While noting the positive developments that had occurred, including the installation of the GURN and the return of UNITA deputies to the National Assembly, the report described the tasks that remained ahead and outlined which aspects of the Lusaka Protocol remained only partially implemented. On the military side, the secretary-general said that while over 71,000 UNITA personnel had been registered in the quartering areas, deserters and absentees had reduced that total by 35 percent. Similarly, the number of UNITA troops incorporated into the national army had reached about 11,000 but fell far short of the 26,300 on which the two military commands had agreed. In the absence of further volunteers, the Joint Commission was obliged to declare the closing of the selection process on May 31. The same story applied to the police. While the Lusaka Protocol had earmarked 5,500 police slots for UNITA, only 524 had been selected to join the force.

What accounted for these statistically significant shortcomings? Although the qualifications (age and education) might provide a partial explanation, other considerations were involved. A significant number of UNITA's regular troops, who would normally have constituted the core group for incorporation, remained outside the quartering areas. Also important were the instructions that the UNITA troops received from their commanding officers. During a visit to the N'tuco quartering area in Zaire province in November 1996, I met with a contingent of UNITA troops who had just come from Cabinda. I asked one soldier if he intended to join the national army or return to his village. The soldier cryptically replied that would depend on the instructions he received! I could only surmise that UNITA's high command had set its own quotas on the numbers to be incorporated into the army and police.

Other outstanding military issues concerned the dismantling of UNITA's command posts and the provision of accurate information on the strength of and weapons possessed by the presidential guard. The secretary-general reported that while UNITA had declared all of its command posts had been dismantled, it had categorically declined to hand over its communications equipment to UNAVEM. UNITA maintained it needed the communications equipment for party purposes. With regard to the presidential guard, UNITA had not provided any information on its size to UNAVEM; some estimated it comprised five thousand soldiers or more. In addition, an undetermined number of so-called mining police were still stationed in the UNITA-controlled diamond areas. The secretary-general also lamented the slow progress of disarming the civilian population, which contributed to a climate of insecurity in the countryside, especially in Benguela and Huila provinces where members of the Government Civil Defense Corps were reported to be attacking individuals and villages.

The political agenda also remained unfinished. The still-unresolved issues included the status of the UNITA shortwave radio station, the legalization of UNITA as a political party, and the submission by UNITA of a list of its members to be appointed to local government posts. Beyond these problems, one other monumental task needed to be addressed: the extension of state administration.

EXTENSION OF STATE ADMINISTRATION

Ever since its independence and throughout the long years of civil war, Angola has been divided into zones controlled by either the government or UNITA. Although pieces of territory have shifted from one side to the other over the years, the fracturing of Angola has been the dominant characteristic of the country. In addition to its military presence, UNITA implanted an administrative structure and system of social services in the areas under its control, employing its own flag, songs, and rituals, which further widened the physical and psychological gulf separating the Angolan people.

According to the Lusaka Protocol, the extension of state administration, which involved sending government officials and police to municipalities and communes throughout Angola, was to take place once UNITA's military forces had moved into the quartering areas. At UNITA's request, this timetable was subsequently delayed until the GURN had been formed. The Lusaka Protocol also stipulated that the process would be done cooperatively and would not be imposed by the government. In this spirit, UNITA teachers, health workers, and local administrators would be incorporated into the governmental structures to the greatest possible extent. The 150 state administrative positions allocated to UNITA—from governors to commune administrators—would also be part of this process.

The Joint Commission later elaborated on these principles by describing the methodology for extending state authority. This jointly agreed-on document recognized that the process would be complex and would encounter numerous psychological and logistical difficulties. Its application would require pragmatism and flexibility. Specific issues, including marriage and divorce documents, death certificates, vehicle registration, and property titles, were addressed. The parties agreed that the process would be carried out over a period of three months.

The framework document did not specify where the process would begin. UNITA favored beginning the extension of state administration in less sensitive areas, while the government wanted to start in traditional UNITA strongholds. It was finally decided to start the process in M'banza Congo (Zaire province), the only provincial capital that remained under UNITA control. On April 30, 1997, the governor and other provincial authorities were inducted into office in a ceremony witnessed by representatives of the government, UNITA, UNAVEM, and the three observer states.

Although the process got off to a relatively smooth start, it soon ran into problems. The Ministry of Territorial Administration, the overall coordinating body, issued a communiqué on May 19, charging UNITA with delaying the process; it warned that the extension of state administration would continue *with or without* UNITA's participation.[3] The government added that UNITA's delaying tactics could lead to local problems, implying that armed conflicts might occur. Although UNITA complained about the implied use of force, the process resumed on May 26, then was halted several days later when a local UNITA crowd attacked Isaias Samakuva, the chief UNITA delegate to the Joint Commission, during a ceremony in Quibala, Cuanza Sul province. Samakuva was beaten up and briefly hospitalized. There was little doubt that the attack had been organized. The government was certainly convinced this was the case:

> They [the attacks] should not only be viewed as a sign of intolerance by some militants but also as premeditated actions aimed at preventing the implementation of the program for the extension of state administration in areas still under UNITA control.[4]

The attack might also have been intended to send a message to the UNITA representatives in Luanda to watch their step. It was not a good omen.

DIAMONDS

Closely linked to the extension of state administration is the issue of diamonds, the most valuable resource in Angola next to oil. Diamonds provided the financial wherewithal for UNITA to fuel its war machine in the same way that oil provided revenues to the government. Although not all of the diamond-mining areas are controlled by UNITA, many of the richest areas are, particularly those in the Luzamba region (Lunda Norte province), which UNITA seized following the September 1992 elections. According to industry sources, UNITA has received up to $400 million per year from the sale of diamonds. Savimbi publicly claimed that UNITA controls two-thirds of diamond production in Angola.

The Lusaka Protocol did not address the diamond issue. In a strictly legal sense, UNITA was obliged to withdraw its military presence from the diamond areas as part of the quartering and disarming process. But it was understood that this issue would have to be resolved in direct talks between the two parties and that if an understanding were not reached, war might erupt in the Lundas and spill over to other parts of the country. It was also argued that UNITA could not be completely cut off from its revenue base if the movement was to play an effective role in a multiparty democratic system, providing a counterweight to the dominant position of the MPLA. Savimbi made this point during a press interview in May 1996:

> For UNITA it [the issue of the diamond regions] is a question of survival. In 1992 the government should have funded our campaign. It did not. We must therefore provide our own means of funding because, one day, there will be new elections and we will have to pay for our campaign.[5]

During the past several years, there have been extensive, if intermittent, discussions behind the scenes between the government and UNITA about the distribution of diamond resources. A memorandum of understanding was signed between the government and UNITA in November 1996, giving UNITA, through its legally recognized holding company, the right to control or to participate in the exploitation of certain diamond areas. The talks have been conducted quietly and out of the limelight; neither side has been particularly eager to bring outsiders into its confidence or to discuss the details of its position. The role of the mediation team has been largely confined to encouraging the two sides to reach an agreement.

Savimbi gave the most extensive public commentary concerning the diamond question to a Portuguese journalist, Mario Ribeiro, in June 1996:

[RIBEIRO:]   I have heard that the president of ENDIAMA [Angola's national diamond company] visited Bailundo. Is this true?

[SAVIMBI:]   It is true but he did not talk to me. He had no business talking to me. I do not enter into talks about stones. I have not sunk so low as to discuss our diamond wells [as heard].

[RIBEIRO:]   Those stones are precious to UNITA.

[SAVIMBI:]   Yes they are, but I have not sunk that low. He had talks with other UNITA officials. I still don't know what they talked about because it was not important enough for me to ask for an immediate report. Yes, he paid a visit. We acknowledge that there are ongoing discussions, very realistic discussions. . . . The fact is, UNITA cannot be left without resources. It cannot. You cannot ask for everything: Let us have your army! Here, have it. Let us have your weapons! Here, have them. Let us have your money! Oh come on, get real! Nobody will accept that.[6]

Angola has the potential to become a world-class diamond producer. At the present time, the situation in the diamond-mining sector is chaotic, reminiscent of scenes out of the American Wild West. If properly organized, the diamond industry could produce revenues of more than $1 billion per year. In addition to readily accessible high-value diamonds found in alluvial deposits in the river systems, Angola has some of the largest kimberlite pipes—the original volcanic eruption of pipes containing diamonds—in the world. Exploitation of these pipes will require substantial capital investment, primarily for power generation, but will result in large, long-life mines. While the diamond issue has major implications for both sides, it should not be viewed as a zero-sum game.

THE "EARTHQUAKE" IN ZAIRE/CONGO

The unexpected often upsets the calculus of diplomacy. In the case of the Angolan peace process, this upset occurred during late 1996 and early 1997. Far away from Angola proper, rebels launched a revolution in the eastern part of Zaire against the regime of President Mobutu. In a remarkably short space of time, the rebel forces swept through the southern part of the country before turning north to capture Kinshasa, the capital of Zaire, in May 1997. Although the regime of President Mobutu had been rotting from within for years, the sudden change in the strategic heart of Africa sent tremors throughout the region.

Why did the rebels win so quickly and decisively? Although many factors were involved, including the lack of resistance from the Zairean army, regional actors, including the Angolan government, played a decisive role. Early in the conflict, the Angolan government contacted the rebel leader, Laurent Kabila, and agreed to a common strategy. The Angolans airlifted a contingent of Kantangese gendarmes, who had been living in Angola after being driven out of Shaba province (Zaire) by Mobutu in the 1960s, to participate in the fighting in the eastern sector. The government provided these troops with military equipment, including heavy weapons, and this force spearheaded the successful offensive against Kisangani, the largest city in the eastern part of the country, which fell to the rebels in the middle of March.

The rebellion might have stopped after the fall of Kisangani if the rebel alliance had not continued to receive substantial outside assistance. Angola's continuing involvement was not hard to understand. For many years, Mobutu had been one of Savimbi's principal allies. UNITA had sent diamonds to Zaire and received in return arms, food, fuel, and medicines. The clandestine supply network was extensive and involved frequent undeclared night flights between Zaire and UNITA-controlled airstrips in Angola. In addition to the UNITA connection, Kinshasa hosted several Cabindan separatist groups and was reported to have assisted certain Bakongo movements in northern Angola. For all of these reasons, the Angolan government wanted its arch enemy to the north ousted and replaced by a more friendly regime with which it would share a common border of 2,600 kilometers.

The question was now: How would the "earthquake" in Zaire affect the peace process in Angola? Many observers believed that this strategic change in the region would compel Savimbi to comply with UNITA's obligations under the Lusaka Protocol. Others thought that the government, buoyed by its success in Zaire and the apparent destruction of UNITA's supply system, would attack UNITA targets in the northeast in order to deprive UNITA of its access to the diamond fields and to deliver a final coup de grace to its adversary.

The latter scenario appeared to be the government's preferred strategy. Beginning in mid-May 1997, the FAA launched an offensive against UNITA-held diamond areas in Lunda Norte province along the northeastern border. Jardo Muekalia, chair of the Center for Democracy in Angola (formerly the Free Angola Information Service), stated, "The unprovoked Angolan Armed Forces (FAA) offensive is the height of folly. It has the potential to unravel all that has been achieved in the peace process over the last two and a half years. It could set back the cause of national reconciliation and democracy for years if it continues."[7] The press release noted that the government and UNITA had recently reached an agreement in principle on UNITA participation in the diamond industry, and this brought into question the government's intentions. It also pointed to the coincidence of the government's offensive and the communiqué issued by the Ministry of Territorial Administration on May 19, mentioned earlier.

The government did not deny it had conducted military operations in the northeast but claimed that the operations were required to secure the border area and to prevent the infiltration of armed Hutu refugees and remnants of Mobutu's army from joining UNITA.[8] The explanation was not entirely convincing. The more likely, or more important, purpose was to put pressure on UNITA. By the end of the month, the battlefield situation had calmed down, though the atmosphere remained tense. Significantly, the FAA did not attempt to capture Luzamba, UNITA's prize diamond area in Lunda Norte province. In view of the government's deeply ingrained distrust of Savimbi, however, the possibility of further military action could not be ruled out if UNITA refused to dismantle its remaining military machine and continued to impede the extension of state administration.

UNAVEM PHASEDOWN

By the middle of 1997, the UNAVEM III mission was winding down. At the beginning of June, the military component of UNAVEM III stood at 4,700 military personnel, down from a peak level of over 7,000 in 1995.[9] The remaining infantry units were scheduled to be completely phased out by September.[10] Recognizing that a continued UN presence was still required, the Security Council approved the follow-on United Nations Observer Mission in Angola (MONUA). MONUA was initially established for seven months, after which it too was scheduled to be phased out, depending on the circumstances on the ground. The observer mission was authorized to employ over one thousand personnel at a cost of $65 million. While the number of military observers would be reduced from 350 to 86, the police contingent would increase from 260 to 345. In addition, political and human rights staffs would be strengthened and deployed to the field.

During the two and a half years of UNAVEM III, significant changes had occurred inside Angola. Whereas a thousand persons had been dying per day from war-related causes before 1995, Angola had enjoyed relative stability during the ensuing two and a half years. The cease-fire had basically held. Some primary lines of communication had been demined and bridges repaired, allowing somewhat greater circulation of people and goods. The humanitarian catastrophe had diminished. The Joint Commission had provided an important forum for resolving problems and disputes. Nine UNITA generals had joined the FAA; eleven thousand UNITA troops had been incorporated into the national army. The Government of National Unity and Reconciliation had been formed with eleven UNITA officials. Seventy UNITA deputies had rejoined the National Assembly. The demobilization process had started.

The negatives weighed heavily on the opposite side. The level of distrust between the MPLA and UNITA remained high. Savimbi's absence from the swearing-in ceremony symbolized this friction, as did the continuing propaganda campaigns carried out by both sides. Angola's economy was in shambles; its infrastructure and social services were devastated. UNITA retained a military force capable of fighting a guerrilla war in the countryside and the cities. The government estimated UNITA had up to thirty-five thousand troops in the field. The diamond issue had not been finally resolved. The country remained divided into government- and UNITA-controlled areas.

In sum, the Angolan peace process continued to be plagued by crises. There was a nagging sense of incompletion and of suspension between war and peace. At the same time, if looked at from the dark days of 1993–94, the picture seemed somewhat brighter. Neither side wanted to return to war. Peace still seemed within reach.

9

■+■+■

Final
Observations

Diplomacy is an art, not a science. There are no magical pre-scriptions that are easily transferable from one situation to the next. The ineffable qualities of judgment, timing, perseverance, experience, and common sense are generally the key ingredients for a successful diplomatic effort. With this in mind, I offer the following observations on the Angolan peace process.

The Past Is Not Just History. Each conflict has its own characteristics and history. Angola is no exception. The Lusaka peace process, which began in October 1993, did not spring out of the heads of the negotiators but was stitched together from the threads of previous peace initiatives. In order to understand the Lusaka Protocol of 1994, we must look back to the Bicesse Accords of 1991 and to what happened during the elections in September 1992. The elections fundamentally altered the parameters for future peace negotiations, as they were judged to be fair by the international community and thus legitimized the MPLA government in Luanda. While in some ways it might have been easier to start from scratch in Lusaka, this was not an option.

The Question of "Ripeness." Within the field of conflict resolution theory, the proposition has been advanced that a conflict situation has to be "ripe" or that the parties should be experiencing a "hurting stalemate" in order for outside mediation to have some chance of success. While these concepts are interesting and have some relevance, the problem remains of how to determine whether a specific situation is "ripe" or if a "hurting stalemate" actually exists. In some cases, the situation may be very clear. For example, if we look at the complexities—internal and external—that characterize Afghanistan in 1998, the outlook for external intervention and mediation does not look promising. But in most cases it is far more likely that the assessment will be murky and compounded by a lack of reliable information available to policymakers. Angola fit into this category. If anything, most observers at the outset pronounced that the prospects for successfully concluding the Lusaka negotiations were minimal to nonexistent. Even when the negotiations were successfully completed, the prognosis remained negative, casting doubt on the wisdom of investing substantial resources into this particular peace process.

When one descends from the level of theory to the more practical task of dealing with specific situations on the ground, more often than not one discovers that there is no clearly delineated road map —that, indeed, there are few if any road signs at all. This is the real world for policymakers and diplomats.

Importance of a Single Point of Mediation. The Lusaka process was led by the United Nations. Although the choice of mediator or mediators will vary depending on the circumstance, it is imperative to have a single leader or core leadership group. This applies to any conflict situation. For example, if other actors vied with the United States for the leadership role over the Middle East peace process— something that is occasionally bruited about—the result would surely be a loss of direction and control.

In the case of Angola, a supporting cast consisting of Portugal, Russia, and the United States worked closely with the UN special representative, but the observers never tried to supplant his efforts. As I told the Security Council in May 1994, Maître Beye was our captain; we were his lieutenants. This choice of mediator is crucial and can spell the difference between success and failure. In the Lusaka peace process, Beye's diplomatic experience, intelligence, unflagging energy, and tenacity made him an outstanding choice. His African antecedents were also important for providing better understanding of the motivations and sensitivities of the two parties to the conflict.

The problem with having multiple mediators or negotiators was demonstrated when regional actors were brought into the Lusaka process. While the regional actors supported the UN-led effort, complications arose whenever they became too intimately involved in the discussions. During the negotiations, the visit of the Zambian team to Huambo in July 1994 created the impression that there was a separate Zambian initiative to resolve the question of which positions UNITA would occupy in the government. Likewise, the effort to involve Nelson Mandela of South Africa in persuading Jonas Savimbi of UNITA to accept the mediation proposals backfired. Although this step was taken at the initiative of the mediators in order to break an impasse in the negotiations, UNITA tried to use the opportunity to open up another negotiating track, which led only to further delays. Later, during the implementation phase, the South African invitation to Savimbi to visit that country on the eve of the Lusaka summit in late April 1995 almost derailed the meeting between Dos Santos and Savimbi because it was not coordinated with the Angolan government or the mediators. Savimbi's visit to South Africa in January 1997 produced the impression that the South Africans had agreed to negotiate Savimbi's special status in the proposed new government, which again only served to complicate matters. The point is that while it is important to marshal the support of regional and other actors for the peace process, it is critical that the core mediation team remains in full control of the negotiations.

A Seamless Whole. Negotiating and implementing an agreement are inseparable processes. While this point may seem self-evident, it carries certain not-so-obvious implications. It is important to maintain some continuity of personnel between the two phases in order to retain a historical memory of how certain provisions of the peace accords were arrived at and to provide coherence and preserve personal contacts. The latter can be particularly important in the African context. While the negotiator and implementor do not necessarily have to be the same person, this can benefit the process. Again, in the case of Angola it was invaluable to have the same UN special representative during the negotiations and during the implementation phase. Likewise, it helped enormously that the UN deputy force commander who was involved in developing the UN peacekeeping plan had previously served in Angola during the Bicesse period. Continuity within the Troika was also important. The Portuguese ambassador remained in Luanda for more than a year following the negotiations in Lusaka. The American special envoy also remained involved during much of the implementation phase.

The Critical Element of External Intervention. In view of the profound distrust that existed between the two parties, the Lusaka Protocol would never have come to fruition without high-level international intervention. Beye put it this way when he remarked to his Troika colleagues: "It is not certain that the mediators will be able to bring peace to the Angolans, but it is perfectly clear that they will never achieve it without our help." On the other hand, it is equally clear that only the Angolans will be able to achieve peace and reconciliation in their country. External intervention may produce a temporary respite and change the dynamic in a positive direction, but there are finite limits as to what outsiders can do.

The Importance of the United Nations. Although it might be preferable to resolve conflicts through regional or subregional intervention, I doubt that this approach would have succeeded in the Angolan context. Because of the long history of Angola's civil war, many of the African states had been involved or identified with one of the factions at one point or another. It would have been difficult to establish an impartial regional mediation mechanism or to provide the sustained commitment and level of resources required to produce and implement a peace agreement.

The United Nations had the added advantage of being able to bring the full weight of the international community in support of the Lusaka peace process. As was demonstrated during and after the negotiations, both parties were sensitive to the actions of the Security Council. Neither side wanted to be criticized or sanctioned by that body, which gave the mediation team a strong, if somewhat blunt, instrument to push the process along. While this leverage may not exist to the same degree in other conflicts, the United Nations occupies an important position on the world stage, especially in the developing world, which can be effectively employed in crisis situations.

A Matter of Resources. Peacekeeping operations are expensive. Sometimes the expense is lost in the mists of time. How much has the international community spent since 1963 in maintaining a UN presence in Cyprus? How much has the United States spent to keep a battalion at Sharm El Sheik to support the peace treaty between Egypt and Israel? The expenditures for these operations are huge, just as they are huge in Angola. Because of the perceived failure of the United Nations to fund the Bicesse peace process adequately, the Security Council authorized a much larger budget to support the implementation of the Lusaka Protocol. Even so, in an effort to pinch pennies, the United States at one point tried to lessen the burden by asking the Angolan government and UNITA to contribute financially to the peacekeeping expenses. The United States argued that the two adversaries had access to oil and diamond revenues and could afford to make an investment in peace. While this proposition has certain attractions on the surface, it was on the whole dubious; among other things, it would have undermined the independence of the peacekeeping mission. The idea was dropped.

The Collision of Timetables. The timetables of the international community and the Angolans collided throughout the negotiations and during the implementation phase. There is no easy solution to these seemingly irreconcilable differences. Because of the expense, the United Nations needs to impose tight timetables on peacekeeping operations. There has to be a clear "exit" strategy; "mission creep" must be avoided. It is important to avoid giving the impression that the United Nations will remain involved more or less indefinitely, as this can become a political and psychological crutch for the parties. At the same time, it is unrealistic to assume that the wounds of a protracted civil war can be healed quickly.

In the case of Angola, a sustained international commitment will be required for some years to come if the peace process is to succeed in the longer term. When the donor community met in Brussels in September 1995, it sent a powerful signal of its commitment by pledging $1 billion to support Angola's economic rehabilitation. The question remains whether the international community can sustain this level of commitment.

How Effective Were the Peacekeepers? The peacekeepers met most of their objectives. The cease-fire was stabilized. The seven thousand troops deployed throughout the country and successfully protected the quartering areas. While the task was not part of their mandate, the peacekeepers helped to construct the fifteen quartering areas. The accomplishments of the UN engineer units were especially significant. They built or restored more than thirty-eight bridges and demined in excess of 4,500 kilometers of road. We can attribute a large measure of the success of the peacekeeping operation to the planning that was done prior to the arrival of the observers and infantry units.

But there were also problems. With thirty-five nationalities participating in the operation, command, control, and communication difficulties inevitably arose. The machinery of the UN bureaucracy also tended to move slowly, the most glaring example being the late deployment of UN-provided helicopters. It would have been more efficient if fewer countries had been involved. If the UN peacekeeping mission were streamlined to include only two or three countries, far better and quicker results could have been obtained. In the case of Angola, the Indians were especially good because of (a) their professionalism, (b) previous peacekeeping experience, and (c) ability to function effectively in the field without sophisticated First World technologies. At a minimum, the United Nations needs to adopt more stringent criteria for selecting peacekeeping forces. It must also pay greater attention to recruiting language-qualified personnel, especially those serving in observer positions.

The Dynamic between War and Diplomacy. While the international community had a compelling humanitarian imperative to stop the fighting during the negotiations in Lusaka, its calls fell on deaf ears. The reasons are clear. It was unrealistic to expect the government to halt its military buildup or its offensives to capture territory that UNITA had seized following the September 1992 elections. Let us not forget that UNITA was on the verge, or so it seemed, of crushing the MPLA when the civil war resumed at the end of 1992.

The more difficult question to answer is whether the government went too far in carrying out its military offensives against Huambo and Uíge following the initialing of the Lusaka Protocol. The United States thought the offensives imperiled the just-reached peace agreement and questioned whether they materially changed the situation on the ground. An opposite view argued that UNITA would have been even less inclined to honor its obligations under the protocol if it had maintained control over Huambo and Uíge. There is no way to test the validity of the latter thesis. Nor can one judge the degree to which the government's offensives complicated UNITA's willingness or ability to comply with the peace accords.

The only clear fact is that while the dynamics of the battlefield and the changing balance of power between the parties influenced the negotiations, the negotiations also constrained the fighting inside Angola. If the Lusaka Protocol had not been initialed, the government army (FAA) would have continued its offensive against UNITA with uncertain consequences. Since it was unlikely that the FAA would have been able to crush UNITA by force of arms, at least in the near term, Angola would have continued to be devastated by civil war, and at some point, another peace initiative would almost inevitably have been launched with its attendant huge costs and delays.

Amnesty Versus Truth and Justice. The Lusaka Protocol provides for general amnesty for any crimes that may have been committed by any individual during the long course of Angola's civil war. As has been mentioned previously, there was no disagreement between the two parties on this point because both recognized that without this provision, there would have been no peace agreement. Given Angola's bloody history, each side would have accused the other endlessly about specific acts and atrocities committed during the civil war. How could these accusations have possibly been sorted out? Who would have been the judge or judges?

Some have argued, however, that some type of mechanism or procedure—perhaps based on South Africa's Truth and Reconciliation Commission—should have been established to deal with the injustices of the past in order to promote real healing and national reconciliation. At some point, the Angolan people will have to come to grips with what has been their national tragedy and nightmare. In Angola's case, this is more likely to come through the voices of its poets, writers, musicians, and church leaders, rather than through the institution of more formalized procedures that would only deepen the wounds.

The Role of the United States. The United States played a critical, perhaps even decisive, role in the Angolan peace process through its support of the UN-led effort. During the negotiations, the president, National Security Council adviser, and assistant secretary of state for African affairs intervened at critical moments with UNITA and the government to break impasses and move the talks forward. There was strong bipartisan congressional support for the negotiations in Lusaka, which included sending joint letters to Dos Santos and Savimbi whenever events took a dangerous turn. This relative unanimity across party lines was especially important in view of the earlier, sharp disagreements within Congress about U.S. policy toward Angola. When the peace agreement was finally reached, the mutual interest of the administration and Congress in resolving Angola's civil war facilitated the approval of sending a large peacekeeping force during a time when Washington circles were generally looking with disfavor on the United Nations and its peacekeeping operations.

Strong U.S. interest continued during the implementation phase. Two talented and active ambassadors, DeJarnette and Steinberg, spearheaded the effort. In addition to frequent visits by the assistant secretary of state for African affairs and the special envoy, a number of high-ranking administration officials traveled to Angola to demonstrate American commitment to the peace process. They included the secretary of state, the U.S. permanent representative to the United Nations, the director of the Agency for International Development, the deputy commander in chief of the United States European Command, the deputy U.S. permanent representative to the United Nations, and the assistant secretary of state for international organization affairs. Frequent White House, National Security Council, and State Department letters and statements reinforced this sense of high-level engagement. The official visit of President Dos Santos to Washington in December 1995 conveyed the strongest possible message of U.S. determination to make the peace process succeed.

The United States also provided resources to support the peace process. To date, about $350 million in emergency relief assistance has been given to alleviate the humanitarian disaster begun in 1992. At the Brussels Roundtable on Angola in September 1995, the United States pledged $190 million to support reconstruction in Angola over a two-year period. In addition, the United States took on a substantial share of the costs of the peacekeeping mission. By any measure, the United States has invested heavily in the Angolan peace process.

If there is a blight on this record, it has been the failure of the United States to pay its full dues to the United Nations, which has affected the way in which peacekeeping operations are viewed worldwide. While this issue is largely rooted in domestic considerations, it did have an impact on the Angolan operation. Due primarily to American concerns, the Security Council was hesitant to approve sending the infantry units to Angola. Subsequently, budgetary considerations largely dictated the timing of the replacement of UNAVEM III by an observer mission, MONUA. If a greater domestic consensus existed about American financial commitments to the United Nations, which are not that onerous, it would be possible to conduct peacekeeping operations with a more pragmatic view of what is needed on the ground. Instead, there is a tendency to be unduly focused on the bottom line.

But by any measure, American involvement in Angola has been sustained and significant, especially when weighed against American engagement in the rest of Africa. Even more important, the policy has been purposeful and steady in its support of the UN-led effort, despite occasional temptations to second-guess or change the ground rules from afar in Washington. This sense of purpose has provided the key to the success that has been achieved thus far in this case of third-party mediation.

Epilogue

Throughout the summer of 1997, the Angolan peace process continued to sputter. As indicated in the reports of the UN secretary-general and the resolutions of the Security Council, UNITA was chiefly responsible for the slow progress. The major outstanding issues were spelled out in Security Council Resolution 1127, adopted on August 28, 1997, which called on UNITA to demilitarize its forces; transform its radio station, VORGAN, into a nonpartisan broadcasting facility; and cooperate fully in the extension of state administration throughout the territory of Angola. With regard to the last point, five localities still under the control of UNITA were identified as being of special importance: Negage, the site of the principal airport in the north; Cuango, situated in the richest diamond-mining area in the northeast; Bailundo and Andulo, two towns in the central highlands where UNITA's headquarters were located; and Mavinga, located in the southern region.

Security Council Resolution 1127 also spelled out a set of sanctions that would be imposed against UNITA at the end of September 1997 unless UNITA took concrete steps to comply with its obligations under the Lusaka Protocol. The major sanctions included travel restrictions on senior UNITA officials (unless the officials were part of the GURN, National Assembly, or Joint Commission), the closure of UNITA offices overseas, and the prohibition of flights into UNITA-controlled areas.

During a visit to Angola in September 1997, Ambassador Steinberg and I met with Savimbi. We urged him to take immediate steps to facilitate the extension of state administration, in the first instance in Negage and Cuango. We discussed the possibility of cohabitation arrangements in both areas. On the issue of the diamond fields, Savimbi suggested that UNITA retain control over the mining areas for a specified period, after which they would be turned over to the government; he explained that the revenues earned in the interim would enable UNITA to exploit the diamond concessions that had been granted to UNITA by the government. This initiative subsequently led to a side agreement between the government and UNITA concerning the diamond areas and the extension of state administration during September to the towns of Negage and Cuango. The Security Council decided to postpone the imposition of sanctions until the end of October.

When Steinberg and I met with Savimbi in October, the peace process, despite the promise of the previous month, had stalled again. The UNITA leader declared that the government had employed undue military pressure while taking over Negage, making further cohabitation arrangements impossible. The pattern of the excessive use of force against UNITA personnel and structures had also characterized the extension of state administration to other localities. Even more serious, he said, the FAA had moved a regiment toward Cuango, forcing the expatriate diamond miners to flee the area, and thus had violated the agreement that had just been reached. (The government claimed that this action had to be taken because the lives of the government administrators in Cuango had been in severe jeopardy.) Savimbi also criticized the government's military intervention in Congo/Brazzaville in support of former president Sassou and against the elected government of President Pascal Lissouba—though, for its part, the government claimed that this intervention was prompted by Lissouba's support of UNITA. In sum, the mood of the meeting was glum.

The government, meanwhile, was following a two-pronged approach. On the one side, it was seeking increased international pressure against UNITA through the Security Council. On the other side, the government was trying to establish a *cordon sanitaire* along its borders to impede the flow of supplies and equipment to UNITA. Following the overthrow of Mobutu in the former Zaire in May 1997, the government seized the opportunity to intervene militarily in Congo/Brazzaville five months later. The government also acted at the political level to prod Zambia to monitor its border with Angola more effectively. While UNITA's logistical pipeline was not closed down, UNITA found it harder and more expensive to obtain supplies.

Although UNITA was repeatedly warned by Beye, the Americans, and the Troika partners that additional sanctions would fall unless it began to fulfill its remaining commitments, UNITA did not heed the warnings. On October 30, 1997, the sanctions came into effect, prompting UNITA to claim they were unjust and would create enormous difficulties for it in fulfilling its remaining tasks. Only toward the end of November did the process of extending state administration slowly restart. Even so, both sides accused the other of committing gross human rights violations when state administration was extended. According to MONUA, neither party was blameless; excesses had been committed both by the national police and by UNITA militants.

At the beginning of the new year, new hope was instilled in the peace process. Following intensive consultations, including a telephone call from Savimbi to Dos Santos, the Joint Commission approved a new timetable on January 9, 1998, which foresaw the completion of the remaining tasks by February. Much less publicized was the peaceful transfer in early January of the rich Luzamba diamond region to government authority. According to industry sources, these mines accounted for 80 percent or more of UNITA's revenues. Coupled with the steady increase in oil production, the government appeared to be getting the upper hand economically. The transfer of the diamond fields also led to a dramatic decline in the number of flights to UNITA areas.

Like virtually all other timetables, the "final" timetable of January 9 was not met, and yet another calender was adopted on March 6. This time, however, substantial progress was realized. By the middle of April, the UN secretary-general could report that eleven out of the twelve pending tasks listed under the new timetable adopted by the Joint Commission had been completed. They included, inter alia, UNITA's declaration on the demilitarization of its forces; the legalization of UNITA as a political party; the appointment of three UNITA governors and seven vice governors, as well as six ambassadors; the cessation of broadcasts by VORGAN; the promulgation of Savimbi's special status; and the agreement on the security detachment for the UNITA leader. I was present at the airport when UNITA's vice president, Antonio Sebastiao Dembo, accompanied by three senior UNITA officials arrived in Luanda on April 1 to prepare for the establishment of UNITA headquarters in the capital.

When I saw Savimbi during the same trip, we discussed the progress that had been made in fulfilling the peace accords, as well as the tasks that still remained, principally disarming of the civilian population and extending state administration to Andulo and Bailundo. Overall, the tone of the conversation was positive. Savimbi said he did not believe that cohabitation was feasible in Andulo and Bailundo after what had happened in Negage and elsewhere, but otherwise gave no indication that the extension would be blocked. He also foresaw going to Luanda at some point since it was the seat of power, and explained that this was why he had sent Dembo and his team to the capital. I left Angola believing that the formal implementation of the Lusaka Protocol (except for the holding of the second round of presidential elections) would be completed by the end of April.

It was not to be. In fact, the situation on the ground seriously deteriorated in the following weeks, revealing a disjunction between what had been achieved at the formal level and what was actually happening in the countryside. Some of the attacks targeted government institutions and personnel, especially the national police, and had, according to MONUA, the characteristics of an organized military operation identified with UNITA. In many cases, MONUA personnel also came under attack. UNITA predictably denied the charges and, in turn, cited instances of brutality by the government's security forces. UNITA's representatives also pointed to the systematic campaign of hostile propaganda that was being conducted by the government-controlled media. Under these circumstances, UNITA argued that the extension of state administration to Andulo and Bailundo would be impossible to implement.

In the second half of May, Beye decided that the situation was serious enough to warrant a major intervention to break out of the crisis. He developed a plan that assigned specific responsibilities to each of the parties, including the United Nations and himself. The government was asked to restrain the media's negative bias against UNITA and to bring its police forces under firmer control. MONUA (despite its steady downsizing) was instructed to carry out its investigations more expeditiously. UNITA was called on to permit the peaceful extension of state administration to Andulo and Bailundo by the end of May. With respect to himself, Beye threatened to resign if the Angolan parties did not demonstrate the political will to fully implement the Lusaka Protocol.

In response to Beye's last-ditch effort, the government took steps to bring its media and police under better control. UNITA presented a counterproposal that called for the extension of state administration to Andulo and Bailundo by June 25, though it still conditioned its proposal on the government's performance. On June 12, the Security Council adopted Resolution 1173 that would automatically impose a third tranche of economic and financial sanctions against UNITA on June 25 if state administration was not extended to four sensitive sites (Andulo, Bailundo, Mungo, and N'Harea). Subsequently, the Security Council extended the deadline to the end of June.

However, in his report to the Security Council of June 23, the secretary-general expressed alarm about what was happening inside Angola. While the government was not completely absolved, the secretary-general stated that the serious deterioration of the security situation was "attributable, for the most part, to the failure of UNITA to fulfill its obligations under the Lusaka Protocol." He expressed concern that UNITA appeared to have retained a large number of troops. Although not explicitly said, it was clear from the report that Savimbi was preserving his war option, or, at least, the ability to assert UNITA control and influence over substantial areas of the country.

In the early hours of Saturday, June 27, Steinberg called me from Luanda to convey shocking news. A plane carrying Beye and his party had crashed in a mangrove swamp on its approach to Abidjan airport the evening before. I could not believe what Steinberg was saying. I had spoken to Beye on Thursday evening and knew of his plans to visit a number of African capitals to rally support for the completion of the Lusaka Protocol. At that time, I told Beye I was looking forward to seeing him in Luanda the following week. As the reality of what had happened sank in, I realized how serious a blow his death was to the peace process. No one, after all, had given more in trying to bring peace to the Angolan people. Indeed, the stress of being the peacemaker and mediator for almost five years had hurt him physically and had required a major heart operation earlier in the year. Now he had given his life.

At a personal level, I was crushed. I had lost a friend, colleague, and brother. This time, I would be going back to Angola with a heavy heart and a sense of foreboding. I only hoped that Beye's untimely and tragic death would prompt Angola's leaders, most importantly Jonas Savimbi, to rededicate themselves to the cause of peace.

◆ ◆ ◆

This book was originally dedicated to Alioune Blondin Beye for his service in advancing peace in Angola. It is now dedicated to his memory.

Appendix I

━━━━━━━━━━━━━━ ■+■+■ ━━━━━━━

Chronology of
Events, 1975–98

1975

15 January   Alvor Accords signed

11 November   Angolan independence declared

1988

20 December   UNAVEM I established by UN Security Council
                    (Resolution 626)

22 December   Tripartite Accords signed

1991

30 May   UNAVEM II authorized by UN Security Council
                    (Resolution 696)

31 May   Acordos de Paz para Angola (Bicesse Accords) signed

1992

29–30 September   Angolan elections

5 October   Senior UNITA generals resign from the FAA

Late October   Massacres in Luanda; departure of UNITA
                    from Luanda

1993

January–March   Peace talks in Addis Ababa

12 April–31 May   Abidjan talks

25 October   Preliminary talks in Lusaka

15 November   Opening plenary session of Lusaka peace talks

11 December   Kuito/Bié incident; alleged assassination attempt
                    against Savimbi

1994

25 March	First U.S. presidential letter to Dos Santos
23 April	Second U.S. presidential letter to Dos Santos
28 May	Government accepts "March 17 proposals"
14 June	First U.S. presidential letter to Savimbi
23 June	Mediators meet with President Mandela
5 September	UNITA accepts "May 28 proposals"
31 October	Lusaka Protocol initialed
9 November	Huambo seized by Angolan government
20 November	Lusaka Protocol signed
4 December	First meeting of the Joint Commission in Luanda

1995

8 February	UNAVEM III authorized by UN Security Council (Resolution 976)
25 March	Secretary-general sends letter to the Security Council supporting the sending of peacekeepers to Angola
7 April	Joint Commission meets with Savimbi in Bailundo
6 May	First meeting between Dos Santos and Savimbi in Lusaka
10 August	Second meeting between Dos Santos and Savimbi, Franceville, Gabon
6 September	Brussels roundtable on Angola; third meeting between Dos Santos and Savimbi
20 November	Process of quartering UNITA forces launched
29 November– 4 December	Angolan government attacks around Soyo
8 December	Dos Santos pays official visit to Washington

1996

18–20 January	Albright, U.S. ambassador to the UN, visits Angola
1 March	Fourth meeting between Dos Santos and Savimbi, Libreville, Gabon
11 December	Completion of UNITA troop quartering process; UNITA generals incorporated into the FAA
20 December	UNITA generals take oath of office

1997

22–25 March	Visit to Angola by UN Secretary-General Annan
9 April	UNITA deputies sworn into National Assembly
11 April	Government of National Unity and Reconciliation inaugurated
1 July	MONUA authorized by UN Security Council (Resolution 1118)
28 August	Security Council threatens to impose second set of sanctions (Resolution 1127) on UNITA at end of September
29 October	Security Council imposes additional sanctions on UNITA (Resolution 1135)

1998

Early January	Transfer of Luzamba diamond areas to government control
12 June	Security Council threatens UNITA with third set of sanctions (Resolution 1173) by June 25 unless state administration extended to Andulo, Bailundo, and two other sensitive sites

Appendix II

■·■·■

UN Security Council Resolutions, 1978–98

Resolution 435 (1978): establishes settlement plan for Namibia

Resolution 626 (20 December 1988): establishes UNAVEM I

Resolution 696 (30 May 1991): establishes UNAVEM II

Resolution 785 (30 October 1992): supports September elections as "generally free and fair"

Resolution 834 (1 June 1993): condemns UNITA for continuation of war

Resolution 864 (15 September 1993): calls UNITA's actions a "threat to international peace and security"; issues first threat of sanctions against UNITA (first against nonstate)

Resolution 922 (31 May 1994): welcomes acceptance of proposals by Angolan government

Resolution 932 (30 June 1994): welcomes acceptance of proposals by UNITA

Resolution 952 (27 October 1994): authorizes restoration of UNAVEM II to previous levels

Resolution 976 (8 February 1995): establishes UNAVEM III

Resolution 1045 (8 February 1996): expresses concern over slow process of UNITA quartering and extends the UNAVEM mandate for three months

Resolution 1075 (11 October 1996): expresses disappointment in UNITA delays and readiness to enact trade measures against UNITA

Resolution 1087 (11 December 1996): authorizes gradual withdrawal of UNAVEM III

Resolution 1102 (31 March 1997): considers imposition of measures against UNITA if GURN is not installed by 11 April 1997

Resolution 1106 (16 April 1997): welcomes inauguration on GURN on 11 April; requests secretary-general to complete withdrawal of UNAVEM III; will consider establishment of a "follow-on" mission for UN

Resolution 1118 (30 June 1997): establishes MONUA, as of 1 July 1997

Resolution 1127 (28 August 1997): threatens second set of sanctions against UNITA

Resolution 1135 (29 October 197): imposes additional sanctions, including travel restrictions, on UNITA

Resolution 1173 (12 June 1998): threatens third set of sanctions against UNITA

Notes

INTRODUCTION

1. United Nations Security Council, *Further Report of the Secretary-General on the United Nations Angola Verification Mission II (UNAVEM II)*, S/25840, 25 May 1993, 7.

2. Fred Bridgland, *Jonas Savimbi: A Key to Africa* (New York: Paragon House, 1987), 125.

3. The exception to this sense of national identity lies among the people of the northernmost province of Cabinda, geographically separated from the rest of Angola by colonial fiat. Most of Angola's oil resources are located off the shore of this province, making control of Cabinda a rich prize. Various separatist movements operate in the province but have not effectively challenged government authority. Both the government and UNITA consider Cabinda to be an integral part of Angola.

1. A BRIEF HISTORY

1. For an exhaustive study of UNAVEM II, the September 1992 elections, and the bloody aftermath, see Margaret Joan Anstee, *Orphan of the Cold War: The Inside Story of the Collapse of the Angolan Peace Process, 1992–93* (New York: St. Martin's Press, 1996). Anstee was the special representative of the secretary-general of the United Nations for Angola and head of the United Nations Angola Verification Mission from February 1992 to June 1993.

2. TALKS TO BEGIN TALKS

1. Republican Study Committee, "Angola: Salvaging Another UN Peacekeeping Fiasco," U.S. House of Representatives, 13 September 1993, 1.

2. "Envoy to Angola Named," *Washington Post*, 23 October 1993, A18.

3. UN Security Council Resolution 834, S/RES/834, 1 June 1993.

4. UN Security Council Resolution 864, S/RES/864, 15 September 1993.

5. Jamba Voz da Resistencia do Galo, 14 September 1993, as printed in *FBIS Daily Report: Southern Africa,* FBIS-AFR-93-176, 14 September 1993, 21.

6. "Comunicado Final da Reuniao Extraordinaria da Comissao Politica da UNITA," *Free Angola Information Service,* 6 October 1993.

7. In many cases, the antagonists had different names for the same place; in this case, the government name was Kuito, while the name preferred by UNITA was Bié.

8. President Clinton's letter was issued by the U.S. Department of State, Washington, D.C., 20 October 1993.

9. Official dispatch.

3. MILITARY AND POLICE TALKS

1. The phrase "relentless intensity" was coined by Robert Oakley, as noted by Chester A. Crocker, "Conclusion" in David R. Smock and Chester A. Crocker, eds., *African Conflict Resolution: The U.S. Role in Peacemaking* (Washington, D.C.: United States Institute of Peace Press, 1995),124.

2. See Anstee, *Orphan of the Cold War*; Fen Osler Hampson, *Nurturing Peace: Why Peace Settlements Succeed or Fail* (Washington, D.C.: United States Institute of Peace Press, 1996), 125; and Yvonne C. Lodico, "A Peace That Fell Apart: The United Nations and the War in Angola," in William J. Durch, ed., *UN Peacekeeping, American Politics, and the Uncivil Wars of the 1990s* (New York: St. Martin's Press, 1996), 103–134.

3. Anstee, *Orphan of the Cold War,* 38.

4. Jamba Voz da Resistencia do Galo, 17 March 1994, as printed in *FBIS Daily Report: Southern Africa,* FBIS-AFR-94-053, 18 March 1994, 16.

5. Ibid.

4. THE POLITICAL QUID PRO QUO

1. Lisbon Radio Renascenca, 6 February 1994, as printed in *FBIS Daily Report: Southern Africa,* FBIS-AFR-94-025, 7 February 1994.

2. U.S. Department of State, "White House Press Statement," 10 February 1994.

3. U.S. Department of State, Warren Christopher, "Letter to President Dos Santos," February 18, 1994.

4. Ambassador Botcharnikov replaced Yuri Kapralov as head of the Russian delegation for a period of six months beginning in February 1994.

5. "Letter from the President of the United States to the President of the Republic of Angola," The White House, Washington, D.C., 25 March 1994.

6. "Letter from the President of the Republic of Angola to the President of the United States," Luanda, 28 March 1994.

7. "Letter from the President of the United States to the President of the Republic of Angola," The White House, Washington, D.C., 23 April 1994.

8. "Letter from the President of the Republic of Angola to the President of the United States," Luanda, 5 May 1994.

9. "Letter from the President of the United States to Jonas Savimbi," The White House, Washington, D.C., 14 June 1994.

10. As it turned out, neither the government nor UNITA wanted the South Africans involved in the peacekeeping force. The government objected based on past South African involvement in the Angolan war. UNITA was disinclined because of the South African mercenaries who were now engaged by the Angolan government in the fight against UNITA. Many of the South African mercenaries had previously fought alongside UNITA against the government.

11. UN Security Council, *Report of the Secretary-General on the United Nations Angola Verification Mission (UNAVEM II)*, S/1994/740, 20 June 1994, and S/1994/740/Add.1, 29 June 1994.

12. Official telegram.

13. UN Security Council Resolution 932, S/RES/932, 30 June 1994.

14. "CSIS Analyst Says: Mediation Doesn't Foster Reconciliation," *News* (Free Angola Information Service), 11 July 1994.

15. Letter from Dr. Gerald Bender to U.S. National Security Advisor Anthony Lake, Culver City, California, 17 June 1994.

16. Jamba Voz da Resistencia do Galo, 28 July 1994, as printed in *FBIS Daily Report: Southern Africa*, FBIS-AFR-94-145, 28 July 1994, 9.

17. UN Security Council, *Statement by the President of the Security Council*, S/PRST/1994/45, 12 August 1994.

18. The negotiations on the specific localities to be offered at the municipal and communal levels continued through October. In all, UNITA received 167 positions at the national, provincial, and local levels.

5. THE START OF IMPLEMENTATION

1. UN Security Council, *Report of the Secretary-General on the United Nations Angola Verification Mission (UNAVEM II)*, S/1994/1197, 20 October 1994, 3.

2. Luanda Radio National Network, 19 September 1994, as printed in *FBIS Daily Report: Southern Africa*, FBIS-AFR-94-182, 20 September 1994, 10.

3. Lisbon RDP Antena 1 Radio Network, 19 September 1994, as printed in *FBIS Daily Report: Southern Africa,* FBIS-AFR-94-182, 20 September 1994, 12.

4. Jamba Voz da Resistencia do Galo Negro, 7 October 1994, as printed in *FBIS Daily Report: Southern Africa,* FBIS-AFR-94-196, 11 October 1994, 11.

5. Maputo Radio Mozambique Network, 2 November 1994, as printed in *FBIS Daily Report: Southern Africa,* FBIS-AFR-94-213, 3 November 1994, 12.

6. Lisbon RDP Antena 1 Radio Network, 7 November 1994, as printed in *FBIS Daily Report: Southern Africa,* FBIS-AFR-94-216, 8 November 1994, 8.

7. See UN Security Council Resolution 952, 27 October 1994; and U.S. Department of State, Office of the Spokesman, "Angola: Condemnation of Siege of Uíge," 18 November 1994.

8. Jamba Voz da Resistencia do Galo Negro, 9 November 1994, as printed in *FBIS Daily Report: Southern Africa,* FBIS-AFR-94-217, 9 November 1994, 13.

9. Luanda Radio National Network, 9 November 1994, as printed in *FBIS Daily Report: Southern Africa,* FBIS-AFR-94-218, 10 November 1994, 10.

10. Luanda TPA Television Network, 13 November 1994, as printed in *FBIS Daily Report: Southern Africa,* FBIS-AFR-94-219, 14 November 1994, 9.

11. Luanda TPA Television Network, 14 November 1994, as printed in *FBIS Daily Report: Southern Africa,* FBIS-AFR-94-220, 15 November 1994, 5–6.

12. Lisbon RDP Antena 1 Radio Network, 17 November 1994, as printed in *FBIS Daily Report: Southern Africa,* FBIS-AFR-94-222, 17 November 1994, 9.

13. London BBC World Service, 17 November 1994, as printed in *FBIS Daily Report: Southern Africa,* FBIS-AFR-94-222, 17 November 1994, 9.

14. London BBC World Service, 17 November 1994, as printed in *FBIS Daily Report: Southern Africa,* FBIS-AFR-94-223, 18 November 1994, 23.

15. Ibid., 24.

16. Luanda TPA Television Network, 20 November 1994, as printed in *FBIS Daily Report: Southern Africa,* FBIS-AFR-94-224, 21 November 1994, 8.

17. UN Security Council, *Letter Dated 7 December 1994 from the Secretary-General Addressed to the President of the Security Council,* S/1994/1395, 8 December 1994.

18. All comments from Luanda TPA Television Network, 4 December 1994, as printed in *FBIS Daily Report: Southern Africa,* FBIS-AFR-94-234, 6 December 1994, 19–20.

19. U.S. Department of State, Office of the Spokesman, "Angola: Peace Process," 7 December 1994.

20. Luanda Radio National Network, 9 December 1994, as printed in *FBIS Daily Report: Southern Africa,* FBIS-AFR-94-238, 12 December 1994, 16.

21. Jamba Voz da Resistencia do Galo Negro, 15 December 1994, as printed in *FBIS Daily Report: Southern Africa,* FBIS-AFR-94-241, 15 December 1994, 11.

22. Ibid.

23. London BBC World Service, 14 December 1994, as printed in *FBIS Daily Report: Southern Africa,* FBIS-AFR-94-241, 15 December 1994, 12.

24. Lisbon RTP-2 Television Network, 11 January 1995, as printed in *FBIS Daily Report: Southern Africa,* FBIS-AFR-95-009, 13 January 1994, 8.

25. *Libération* (Paris), 21 December 1994, as printed in *FBIS Daily Report: Southern Africa,* FBIS-AFR-94-246, 22 December 1994, 22–23.

26. Lisbon RDP Antena 1 Radio Network, 21 December 1994, as printed in *FBIS Daily Report: Southern Africa,* FBIS-AFR-94-245, 21 December 1994, 14.

27. Luanda Radio National Network, 21 December 1994, as printed in *FBIS Daily Report: Southern Africa,* FBIS-AFR-94-246, 22 December 1994, 24.

28. Lisbon RTP-2 Television Network, 11 January 1995, as printed in *FBIS Daily Report: Southern Africa,* FBIS-AFR-95-009, 13 January 1995, 10.

29. Luanda Radio National Network, 30 December 1994, as printed in *FBIS Daily Report: Southern Africa,* FBIS-AFR-95-001, 3 January 1995, 13–14.

30. From the author's personal notes.

31. Initially, part of the problem was that the October 27 Security Council resolution (952) authorizing the enlargement of UNAVEM II to its Bicesse levels did not contain a budget for helicopter support. Following the adoption of the February 8 Security Council resolution (976) establishing UNAVEM III, there was a budget, but the helicopter contract became mired in the politics of the UN bureaucracy in New York.

32. Luanda Radio National Network, 11 January 1995, as printed in *FBIS Daily Report: Southern Africa,* FBIS-AFR-95-007, 11 January 1995, 11.

33. UN Security Council, *Report of the Secretary-General on the United Nations Angola Verification Mission (UNAVEM II),* S/1995/97, 1 February 1995, 15.

34. London BBC World Service, 8 February 1995, as printed in *FBIS Daily Report: Southern Africa,* FBIS-AFR-95-026, 8 February 1995, 12; and Luanda TPA Television Network, 9 February 1995, as printed in *FBIS Daily Report: Southern Africa,* FBIS-AFR-95-028, 10 February 1995, 17.

35. London BBC World Service, 8 February 1995, as printed in *FBIS Daily Report: Southern Africa,* FBIS-AFR-95-028, 10 February 1995, 17.

36. Luanda TPA Television Network, 9 February 1995, as printed in *FBIS Daily Report: Southern Africa,* FBIS-AFR-95-028, 10 February 1995, 17.

37. Jamba Voz da Resistencia do Galo Negro, 13 February 1995, as printed in *FBIS Daily Report: Southern Africa,* FBIS-AFR-95-029, 13 February 1995, 10–11.

38. Jamba Voz da Resistencia do Galo Negro, 12 February 1995, as printed in *FBIS Daily Report: Southern Africa,* FBIS-AFR-95-029, 13 February 1995, 10.

39. Luanda Radio National Network, 14 February 1995, as printed in *FBIS Daily Report: Southern Africa,* FBIS-AFR-95-031, 15 February 1995, 11.

40. UN Security Council, *Report of the Secretary-General on the United Nations Angola Verification Mission (UNAVEM II),* S/1995/97, 1 February 1995, 18.

41. From the author's personal notes.

42. UN Security Council, *First Progress Report of the Secretary-General on the United Nations Angola Verification Mission (UNAVEM III),* S/1995/117, 5 March 1995, 2.

43. Luanda TPA Television Network, 20 February 1995, as printed in *FBIS Daily Report: Southern Africa,* FBIS-AFR-95-035, 22 February 1995, 25–26.

44. *Le Monde* (Paris), 16 February 1995, 5, as printed in *FBIS Daily Report: Southern Africa,* FBIS-AFR-95-045, 8 March 1995, 15.

45. Luanda Radio National Network, 18 February 1995, as printed in *FBIS Daily Report: Southern Africa,* FBIS-AFR-95-034, 21 February 1995, 30.

46. London BBC World Service, 24 February 1995, as printed in *FBIS Daily Report: Southern Africa,* FBIS-AFR-95-038, 27 February 1995, 13.

47. See London BBC World Service, 27 February 1995, as printed in *FBIS Daily Report: Southern Africa,* FBIS-AFR-95-039, 28 February 1995, 20; and Jamba Voz da Resistencia do Galo Negro, 28 February 1995, as printed in *FBIS Daily Report: Southern Africa,* FBIS-AFR-95-039, 28 February 1995, 20.

48. London BBC World Service, 15 March 1995, as printed in *FBIS Daily Report: Southern Africa,* FBIS-AFR-95-051, 16 March 1995, 11–12.

49. Jamba Voz da Resistencia do Galo Negro, 16 April 1995, as printed in *FBIS Daily Report: Southern Africa,* FBIS-AFR-95-073, 17 April 1995, 10.

50. I learned the pencil throwing trick from Philip Habib, one of America's finest diplomats. During a particularly stormy meeting with Israeli defense minister Erik Sharon in Jerusalem in December 1981, Habib at one point hurled his pencil on the table in disgust. The technique should only be used in extremis.

51. Luanda Radio National Network, 6 May 1995, as printed in *FBIS Daily Report: Southern Africa,* FBIS-AFR-95-088, 8 May 1995, 12.

52. Ibid.

53. Paul Taylor, "Angolan Civil War Rivals Embrace," *Washington Post*, 7 May 1995, A32.

6. THE ARRIVAL OF THE BLUE HELMETS

1. Harare, Zimbabwe, National Broadcasting Corporation Network, 3 March 1995, as printed in *FBIS Daily Report: Southern Africa*, FBIS-AFR-95-042, 3 March 1995, 12.

2. Luanda Radio National Network, 6 March 1995, as printed in *FBIS Daily Report: Southern Africa*, FBIS-AFR-95-044, 7 March 1995, 6.

3. Lisbon RDP Antena 1 Radio Network, 6 March 1995, as printed in *FBIS Daily Report: Southern Africa*, FBIS AFR-95-044, 7 March 1995, 6.

4. Luanda Radio National Network, 10 March 1995, as printed in *FBIS Daily Report: Southern Africa*, FBIS-AFR-95-048, 13 March 1995, 14.

5. Jamba Voz da Resistencia do Galo Negro, 7 March 1995, as printed in *FBIS Daily Report: Southern Africa*, FBIS-AFR-95-044, 7 March 1995, 7–8.

6. UN Security Council, *Second Progress Report of the Secretary-General on the United Nations Angola Verification Mission (UNAVEM III)*, S/1995/274, 7 April 1995, 7.

7. The agreement was finally signed on May 3, 1995. The main sticking point was the establishment of a UN radio station in Angola. The government argued that its laws prohibited private shortwave radio stations, thus joining the question of the UN radio station to the legal status of UNITA's shortwave radio, VORGAN. The UN radio station was never established, despite frequent demands from the Security Council, though the government did provide UNAVEM with frequencies and time slots on the government-controlled radio station.

8. UN Security Council, *Statement by the President of the Security Council*, S/PRST/1995/11, 10 March 1995, 2.

9. UN Security Council, *Letter Dated 25 March 1995 from the Secretary-General Addressed to the President of the Security Council*, S/1995/230, 28 March 1995, 2.

10. Mechem demined 4,500 kilometers of roads before its contract expired. At first, the company had difficulties obtaining the necessary clearances from the government. Subsequently, UNITA prevented the company from operating in some of its areas.

11. UN Security Council, *Report of the Secretary-General on the United Nations Angola Verification Mission (UNAVEM III)*, S/1995/1012, 7 December 1995, 2.

12. With the arrival of the Ukrainian bridging company, two additional platoons of the Portuguese logistic unit, and the Zambian mechanized company, the full complement of the UNAVEM military component was reached in March 1996. At that time, the force level, including military and police observers, was over seven thousand, making UNAVEM III the largest UN peacekeeping force in the world.

13. CREA Angola Documentation Unit, *Angola Quartering Process: Taking Stock, One Year after the Lusaka Accords* (Washington, D.C.: Creative Associates International, 1995), 17–18.

14. *Guardian* (London), 1 August 1995, 10, as printed in *FBIS Daily Report: Southern Africa*, FBIS-AFR-95-147, 1 August 1995, 8–9.

15. Luanda Radio National Network, 12 September 1995, as printed in *FBIS Daily Report: Southern Africa*, FBIS-AFR-95-177, 13 September 1995, 12.

16. Jamba Voz da Resistencia do Galo Negro, 10 September 1995, as printed in *FBIS Daily Report: Southern Africa*, FBIS-AFR-95-175, 11 September 1995, 20.

17. Although it was agreed that the overall size of the FAA would be 90,000 (army, 74,000; air force, 11,000; and navy, 5,000), the parties disagreed about how many troops UNITA would contribute to the army. UNITA wanted to follow the Bicesse principle of parity, which would entail contributing 37,000 men. The government was opposed and initially offered 17,000 slots. According to the Lusaka Protocol, UNITA had the stronger legal position. Finally, the two sides compromised on 26,300 UNITA troops, including small contributions to the air force (200) and navy (100).

Under the global incorporation concept, all of UNITA's troops would be incorporated into the armed services during a transitional phase and would be gradually demobilized until the overall force ceiling of 90,000 was reached. The government advocated this approach, in part because it would offer greater control over the UNITA military. UNITA was never very enthusiastic about the proposal. Because of its costs, it also did not receive the support of the international community. The plan was finally abandoned.

18. UN Security Council, *Report of the Secretary-General on the United Nations Angola Verification Mission (UNAVEM III)*, S/1995/1012, 7 December 1995, 7.

19. Jamba Voz da Resistencia do Galo Negro, 5 December 1995, as printed in *FBIS Daily Report: Southern Africa*, FBIS-AFR-95-234, 6 December 1995, 8.

20. Luanda TPA Television Network, 18 January 1996, as printed in *FBIS Daily Report: Southern Africa*, FBIS-AFR-96-013, 19 January 1996, 11.

21. Jamba Voz da Resistencia do Galo Negro, 19 January 1996, as printed in *FBIS Daily Report: Southern Africa*, FBIS-AFR-96-014, 22 January 1996, 12.

22. Luanda Radio National Network, 20 January 1996, as printed in *FBIS Daily Report: Southern Africa*, FBIS-AFR-96-014, 22 January 1996, 13.

23. London BBC World Service, 8 February 1996, as printed in *FBIS Daily Report: Southern Africa*, FBIS-AFR-96-028, 9 February 1996, 18.

24. UN Security Council Resolution 1045, 8 February 1996.

25. UN Security Council, *Report of the Secretary-General on the United Nations Angola Verification Mission (UNAVEM III)*, S/1996/171, 6 March 1996, 3.

26. UN Security Council, *Report of the Secretary-General on the United Nations Angola Verification Mission (UNAVEM III)*, S/1996/171, 6 March 1996, 3–4.

27. *Expresso* (Lisbon), 24 February 1996 (p. 20), as printed in *FBIS Daily Report: Southern Africa*, FBIS-AFR-96-041, 29 February 1996, 10.

28. UN Security Council, *Report of the Secretary-General on the United Nations Angola Verification Mission (UNAVEM III)*, S/1996/328, 30 April 1996, 4.

29. Luanda Radio National Network, 24 April 1996, as printed in *FBIS Daily Report: Southern Africa*, 24 April 1996.

30. Luanda Radio National Network, 23 April 1996, as printed in *FBIS Daily Report: Southern Africa*, 23 April 1996.

31. London BBC World Service, 24 April 1996, as printed in *FBIS Daily Report: Southern Africa*, 24 April 1996.

32. U.S. Department of State, *Explanation of Vote: UN Security Council Resolution 1055*, 6 May 1996.

33. UN Security Council, *Report of the Secretary-General on the United Nations Angola Verification Mission (UNAVEM III)*, S/1996/503, 27 June 1996, 3.

34. UN Security Council Resolution 1064, S/RES/1064, 11 July 1996.

35. UN Security Council, *Progress Report of the Secretary-General on the United Nations Angola Verification Mission (UNAVEM III)*, S/1996/827, 4 October 1996, 4.

36. UN Security Council, *Report of the Secretary-General on the United Nations Angola Verification Mission (UNAVEM III)*, S/1997/248, 25 March 1997, 3.

37. The original military accord was signed on March 9 by General João de Matos (FAA) and General Augusto Lutock Liahuka Wiyo (FALA). The agreement stipulated that eighteen UNITA generals would be incorporated into the FAA, as well as a number of other posts from the corporal to colonel levels. However, nine of the slots at the officer rank of general were reserved for the Fourth Branch, which would incorporate all UNITA troops and engage in public works projects. When the concepts of "global incorporation" and the Fourth Branch were dropped at the insistence of UNITA, the number of reserved slots for UNITA generals reverted back to nine.

38. UN Security Council Resolution 1087, 11 December 1996.

7. THE POLITICAL DENOUEMENT

1. Paris AFB, 1 March 1996, as printed in *FBIS Daily Report: Southern Africa*, on CD-ROM disc, "FBIS Publications, Jan. 96–Mar. 96, Disc No. 11."

2. Luanda TPA Television Network, 10 March 1996, as printed in *FBIS Daily Report: Southern Africa*, FBIS-AFR-96-048.

3. Johannesburg Channel Africa Radio, 8 July 1995, as printed in *FBIS Daily Report: Southern Africa*, FBIS-AFR-95-131, 10 July 1995, 11.

4. Paris Radio France International, 11 July 1995, as printed in *FBIS Daily Report: Southern Africa*, FBIS-AFR-95-133, 12 July 1995, 9.

5. Lisbon RDP Antena 1 Radio Network, 10 March 1996, as printed in *FBIS Daily Report: Southern Africa*, FBIS-AFR-96-048.

6. Luanda Radio National Network, 15 March 1996, as printed in *FBIS Daily Report: Southern Africa*, FBIS-AFR-96-053.

7. London BBC World Service, 21 August 1996, as printed in *FBIS Daily Report: Southern Africa*, FBIS-AFR-96-164.

8. Jamba Voz da Resistencia do Galo Negro, 28 August 1996, as printed in *FBIS Daily Report: Southern Africa*, FBIS-AFR-96-168.

9. Lisbon RDP Antena 1 Radio Network, 27 August 1996, as printed in *FBIS Daily Report: Southern Africa*, FBIS-AFR-96-168.

10. Luanda TPA Television Network, 4 September 1996, as printed in *FBIS Daily Report: Southern Africa*, FBIS-AFR-96-173.

11. UNITA, "Status of the President of the Majority Opposition Party (Angola)," 20 September 1996.

12. Government of Angola, "Peace Process Coordinating Body: Special Status Guaranteed to the President of UNITA," 14 November 1996.

13. Johannesburg SAPA, 10 January 1997, as printed in *FBIS Daily Report: Southern Africa*, FBIS-AFR-97-007.

14. Luanda TPA Television Network, 10 January 1997, as printed in *FBIS Daily Report: Southern Africa*, FBIS-AFR-97-008.

15. Johannesburg SAfm Radio Network, 22 January 1997, as printed in *FBIS Daily Report: Southern Africa*, FBIS-AFR-97-015.

16. UN Security Council, *Report of the Secretary-General on the United Nations Angola Verification Mission (UNAVEM III)*, S/1997/115, 7 February 1997, 2.

17. UN Security Council Resolution 1087, S/RES/1087, 11 December 1996.

18. Kwacha UNITA Press WWW (Internet), 13 January 1997, as printed in *FBIS Daily Report: Southern Africa,* FBIS-AFR-97-009.

19. UN Security Council, *Statement by the President of the Security Council,* S/PRST/1997/3, 30 January 1997.

20. Jamba Voz da Resistencia do Galo Negro, 6 February 1997, as printed in *FBIS Daily Report: Southern Africa,* FBIS-AFR-97-025.

21. Luanda Radio National Network, 6 February 1997, as printed in *FBIS Daily Report: Southern Africa,* FBIS-AFR-97-025.

22. UN Security Council, *Statement by the President of the Security Council,* S/PRST/1997/3, 30 January 1997.

23. UN Security Council Resolution 1098, S/RES/1098, 27 February 1997.

24. UN Security Council, *Report of the Secretary General on the United Nations Angola Verification Mission (UNAVEM III),* S/1997/239, 19 March 1997, 2.

25. Luanda Radio National Network, 22 March 1997, as printed in *FBIS Daily Report: Southern Africa,* FBIS-AFR-97-081.

26. UN Security Council, *Report of the Secretary General on the United Nations Angola Verification Mission (UNAVEM III),* S/1997/239, 19 March 1997, 1.

27. Luanda National Radio Network, 31 March 1997, as printed in *FBIS Daily Report: Southern Africa,* FBIS-AFR-97-090.

28. Luanda TPA Television Network, 1 April 1997, as printed in *FBIS Daily Report: Southern Africa,* FBIS-AFR-97-063.

29. London BBC World Service, 2 April 1997, as printed in *FBIS Daily Report: Southern Africa,* FBIS-AFR-97-092.

30. London BBC World Service, 8 April 1997, as printed in *FBIS Daily Report: Southern Africa,* FBIS-AFR-97-098.

31. Luanda TPA Television Network, 11 April 1997, as printed in *FBIS Daily Report: Southern Africa,* FBIS-AFR-97-071.

32. Abidjan La Chaine Une Television Network, 24 April 1997, as printed in *FBIS Daily Report: Southern Africa,* FBIS-AFR-97-11.

33. Lynne Duke, "Angola's Longtime Enemies Completing Peace Process," *New York Times,* 10 April 1997, A28.

8. THE UNFINISHED AGENDA

1. UN Security Council Resolution 1118, S/RES/1118, 30 June 1997.

2. UN Security Council, *Report of the Secretary-General on the United Nations Angola Verification Mission (UNAVEM III),* S/1997/438, 5 June 1997.

3. Luanda Radio National Network, 20 May 1997, as printed in *FBIS Daily Report: Southern Africa,* FBIS-AFR-97-140.

4. Luanda Radio National Network, 1 June 1997, as printed in *FBIS Daily Report: Southern Africa,* FBIS-AFR-97-152.

5. *Le Figaro* (Paris), 15 May 1996, as printed in *FBIS Daily Report: Southern Africa,* FBIS-AFR-96-096.

6. Lisbon Radio Renascenca, 27 June 1996, as printed in *FBIS Daily Report: Southern Africa,* 1 July 1996.

7. Center for Democracy in Angola, "Angolan Army Launches Unprovoked Attacks, Occupies Positions in Lunda Diamond Area," *News,* 23 May 1997.

8. Luanda TPA Television Network, 17 May 1997, as printed in *FBIS Daily Report: Southern Africa,* FBIS-AFR-97-137; and Goodson Machona, "Angola Did Not Fight in Zaire, Insists Envoy," *Lusaka Post* (Internet version), 23 May 1997, as printed in *FBIS Daily Report: Southern Africa,* FBIS-AFR-97-143.

9. UN Security Council, S/1997/438, 5 June 1997, 3.

10. UN Security Council, S/1997/438, add. 1, 5 June 1997, 10.

Selected
Bibliography

Anstee, Margaret Joan. *Orphan of the Cold War: The Inside Story of the Collapse of the Angolan Peace Process, 1992–93.* New York: St. Martin's Press, 1996.

Bender, Gerald J. *Angola under the Portuguese: The Myth and the Reality.* Berkeley: University of California Press, 1978.

Bridgland, Fred. *Jonas Savimbi: A Key to Africa.* New York: Paragon House, 1987.

Collelo, Thomas, ed. *Angola: A Country Study.* 3rd ed. Washington, D.C.: Superintendent of Documents, 1991.

CREA Angola Documentation Unit. *Angola Quartering Process: Taking Stock, One Year after the Lusaka Accords.* Washington, D.C.: Creative Associates International, 1995.

Crocker, Chester A. *High Noon in Southern Africa: Making Peace in a Tough Neighborhood.* New York: W. W. Norton, 1993.

Free Angola Information Service. *News.* Washington, D.C.: Free Angola Information Service, 1994.

Hampson, Fen Osler. *Nurturing Peace: Why Peace Settlements Succeed or Fail.* Washington, D.C.: United States Institute of Peace Press, 1996.

Henderson, Lawrence W. *Angola: Five Centuries of Conflict.* Ithaca: Cornell University Press, 1979.

Hume, Cameron. *Ending Mozambique's War: The Role of Mediation and Good Offices.* Washington, D.C.: United States Institute of Peace Press, 1994.

Maier, Karl. *Angola: Promises and Lies.* London: Serif, 1996.

Smock, David R., and Chester A. Crocker, eds. *African Conflict Resolution: The U.S. Role in Peacemaking.* Washington, D.C.: United States Institute of Peace Press, 1995.

Zartman, I. William. *Ripe for Resolution: Conflict and Intervention in Africa.* Rev. ed. New York: Oxford University Press, 1989.

Index

Paul Hare served for thirty-one years in the Foreign Service, most recently as senior deputy assistant secretary of state at the Bureau of Near Eastern and South Asian Affairs. He was the director of the Office of Southern African Affairs in the State Department from 1979 to 1981. Overseas assignments included Kuwait, Tunisia, Vietnam, Australia, Morocco, and Israel. During his service as U.S. ambassador to Zambia (1985–88), he initiated a high-level dialogue with the headquarters in exile of the African National Congress (South Africa), the first such talks to be conducted at the ambassadorial level.

Hare was named the U.S. special envoy for the Angolan peace process in October 1993. He was one of the participants in the negotiations that led to the signing of the Lusaka Protocol in November 1994. He made a number of trips to Angola in conjunction with the implementation of the peace accords.

Hare is the author of *Diplomatic Chronicles of the Middle East: A Biography of Ambassador Raymond A. Hare.* While a fellow at the United States Institute of Peace (1996–97), he researched and wrote on the Angolan peace process. From 1991 until 1998 he was vice director of the Middle East Institute; he is now executive director of the United States–Angola Chamber of Commerce. Hare received his B.A. degree from Swarthmore College and studied international relations at the University of Chicago.

United States Institute of Peace

The United States Institute of Peace is an independent, nonpartisan federal institution created by Congress to promote research, education, and training on the peaceful resolution of international conflicts. Established in 1984, the Institute meets its congressional mandate through an array of programs, including research grants, fellowships, professional training programs, conferences and workshops, library services, publications, and other educational activities. The Institute's Board of Directors is appointed by the President of the United States and confirmed by the Senate.

Chairman of the Board: Chester A. Crocker
Vice Chairman: Max M. Kampelman
President: Richard H. Solomon
Executive Vice President: Harriet Hentges

Board of Directors

Chester A. Crocker (Chairman), Research Professor of Diplomacy, School of Foreign Service, Georgetown University

Max M. Kampelman, Esq. (Vice Chairman), Fried, Frank, Harris, Shriver and Jacobson, Washington, D.C.

Dennis L. Bark, Senior Fellow, Hoover Institution on War, Revolution and Peace, Stanford University

Theodore M. Hesburgh, President Emeritus, University of Notre Dame

Seymour Martin Lipset, Hazel Professor of Public Policy, George Mason University

W. Scott Thompson, Professor of International Politics, Fletcher School of Law and Diplomacy, Tufts University

Allen Weinstein, President, Center for Democracy, Washington, D.C.

Harriet Zimmerman, Vice President, American Israel Public Affairs Committee, Washington, D.C.

Members ex officio

Richard A. Chilcoat, Lieutenant General, U.S. Army; President, National Defense University

Ralph Earle II, Deputy Director, U.S. Arms Control and Disarmament Agency

Phyllis Oakley, Assistant Secretary of State for Intelligence and Research

Walter B. Slocombe, Under Secretary of Defense for Policy

Richard H. Solomon, President, United States Institute of Peace (nonvoting)

Jennings Randolph Program for International Peace

This book is a fine example of the work produced by senior fellows in the Jennings Randolph fellowship program of the United States Institute of Peace. As part of the statute establishing the Institute, Congress envisioned a program that would appoint "scholars and leaders of peace from the United States and abroad to pursue scholarly inquiry and other appropriate forms of communication on international peace and conflict resolution." The program was named after Senator Jennings Randolph of West Virginia, whose efforts over four decades helped to establish the Institute.

Since 1987, the Jennings Randolph Program has played a key role in the Institute's effort to build a national center of research, dialogue, and education on critical problems of conflict and peace. More than a hundred senior fellows from some thirty nations have carried out projects on the sources and nature of violent international conflict and the ways such conflict can be peacefully managed or resolved. Fellows come from a wide variety of academic and other professional backgrounds. They conduct research at the Institute and participate in the Institute's outreach activities to policymakers, the academic community, and the American public.

Each year approximately fifteen senior fellows are in residence at the Institute. Fellowship recipients are selected by the Institute's board of directors in a competitive process. For further information on the program, or to receive an application form, please contact the program staff at (202) 457-1700.

Joseph Klaits
Director